BITE SIZE

AN ANTHOLOGY OF MICRO THEATRE

A Denver Center for the Performing Arts Off-Center Anthology of Micro Plays by Colorado Playwrights

bookb... press

Denver, Colorado

Paperback: 978-1-7339887-2-8
Ebook: 978-1-7339887-3-5

First paperback edition: December 2020

Cover art by Denver Center for the Performing Arts

Printed by BookBar Press in the USA

BookBar Press
4280 Tennyson Street
Denver, Colorado 80212

www.bookbarpress.com

Public Service Announcement

by Theo E.J. Wilson

I see public servants forgetting their roles. Abusing their power.
Acting like kings. How often they forget:

A king ain't nothin' but a slave with connections
And is only lent his power for his aptitude for service. The
constituents within the body politic
can sever said connections like blood vessels
if the heart becomes perverted…

'Cause it no longer serves its purpose.

When palpitations pump impurities, it poisons precious pathways
and the 'System' faces failure.
And it reacts with an immunity to preserve cell tissue 'communities'

and the illness that ensues is diagnosed…as a rebellion! To those
power-corrupted vessels of oppression…

What will you do when the people have electricity in their eyes
because the scars over their hearts are shaped like voting machines?

Will you finally see that we are One when our hands are around
your necks

And that we share the same air that you're now choking to
breathe?

Whether you know it or not, there is a revolution at hand and
you're in it. They tried to say our revolution was dead —

But how can you tell me Black liberation died
When Assata Shakur is under my tongue?!
But by the time these words hit you mothafuckas, it's gonna taste
like
Nat Turner's knuckles! Hotter than a slave master boiled in vats
of sugar

When the field-hands overrun the big house,

The African Stands

Ask them dead British soldiers in the mountains of Jamaica
about a marooned slave's will to keep breathing in freedom.

A loud message from the ancestors to the British empire that,
"Queen Nanny sends her regards to your blood-claat queen of
England!"

We are the razor between your toes when you're playing Capoeira.
A slave revolt disguised in dance lest your feet just might get
severed!

But you could cut them both off, and I'd still be running this,
Cause an African will escape on her hands:
Shit, you could turn her world upside down, The African Stands!

Sing a freedom song so clear that it shatters the receiver inside
Dr. King's wire-tapped phone!

Piercing the clouds, then back down,
'til the sound reverberates through the titanium in Claudette's
backbone!

'Til Africans rise up from the Atlantic like goose bumps from
your skin,
lightning flashing like the flame from Fannie's gun!

Burning bright as the eye of God when it banged light through
the void,
As Black as the death of a sun. Stand with us. Stand with us!

TABLE OF CONTENTS

Introduction iv

A Pocket Full of Dandelions 1
by Kristen Adele Calhoun

Holy Couch 17
by Edith Weiss

Marginalia 33
by Jeffrey Neuman

Outside the Room 43
by Theatre Artibus, Grapefruit Lab + Larry Mitchell

Toxoplasmosis 53
by Sean Michael Cummings

Something to Read at the End of the World 77
by Maureen Biermann

The F Word 93
by Claire Caviglia

The Missing Piece 107
by Christina Miller + Addie Levinsky

The Side of the Room 121
by Dakota Hill

Malum 141
by Ashley Rice

About the Contributors 155

INTRODUCTION

In the summer of 2016 I attended a micro theatre performance in San Miguel de Allende, Mexico. When I first entered the quaint building, I was given the option to buy tickets for however many micro performances I wanted to see that night before sitting at the bar where I ordered a glass of wine and some steamy herbed potatoes. As I sat there waiting for my friend to arrive, I observed the bustle in the room as theatregoers came and went between shows. They were all talking about the performance they just saw and the performance they were about to see. It was a small room, which made it hard to avoid conversation with familiar or unfamiliar faces. One of the micro plays that stayed with me the most was a one-man show in a coat closet about illegal border crossings—this piece left quite an impact and helped me see the immigration situation in America from a different perspective. My first micro theatre experience inspired me to explore this form more and I was excited about the possibility of bringing a diverse room of people together in a community setting where we could see some great theatre that provokes conversation all while sipping wine.

Meridith C. Grundei
Creator and Director
Bite-Size: An Evening of Micro Theatre

DCPA Off-Center has always been dedicated to the work of local artists; Meridith's idea for *Bite Size* excites me not only because it is a unique experience for audiences, but also because it showcases the work of Colorado writers. The journey of this production began when we put out an open call for original short plays and performance pieces. The rules were simple: it must be written/created by a Colorado resident, between 10 and 15 minutes long, no more than 3 performers, reference or relate to a work of literature, and take place in a location where there are books.

I didn't know what to expect when we invited the community to write micro plays, and I was amazed at the 213 eligible submissions that came in from 101 Colorado zip codes. The large number of scripts is evidence of our vibrant creative community. It also made the selection process incredibly competitive. Each submission was read by at least three readers in a blind process that ensured the works were judged on their own merits, with the identity of the playwright hidden. The reading and selection committees were amazed by the depth of talent and wonderful diversity of the submissions. I hope you enjoy this tasting of original stories by local playwrights, featuring the five plays we produced at BookBar and five finalists that we love. And thanks to BookBar Press for making this special publication possible!

Charlie Miller
Off-Center Curator
Denver Center for the Performing Arts

A POCKET FULL OF DANDELIONS

by Kristen Adele Calhoun

(It is the third night of the uprising. Colorado's Front Range is unrecognizable. Downtown Denver has been blown to pieces. Roads are impassable. Only the Rocky Mountains remain, steadfast and unchanged. We find ourselves in a dark dusty room—the library of Downtown Denver Detention Center, the Denver jail. A knock outside the door.)

MAJOR

(Emerges from the back room of the jail library, carrying a knife. She is a transgender Black woman in a crisp, dark suit. Her lifelong fight for survival has built her resilience to withstand a moment such as this. She lights a candle and goes to the door. She ain't scared but she also ain't playing.)

MAJOR

Password?

OUTSIDER

It is our duty to fight for our freedom.

MAJOR

It is our duty to win.

OUTSIDER

We must love each other, and support each other.

MAJOR and OUTSIDER

We have nothing to lose but our chains.

(MAJOR drops the knife, puts down the candle and rushes to unlock the door. She can't open it fast enough. The OUTSIDER is ARAMINTA aka MINTY, a Black woman in her thirties dressed in sneakers and clothes that have seen better days. She stumbles into the room.)

MAJOR

Minty! How did you get past the guards?

ARAMINTA

I'll explain that to you later. It's not important right now.

MAJOR

Explain it to me later? If you got past the sheriff's deputies, nothing could be more important.

ARAMINTA

Just hold on, Major.

(MAJOR observes her friend as she locks the door. Since she arrived Minty has been searching around the room and placing items in her bag. MINTY staggers and almost falls. She catches herself before hitting the floor.)

MAJOR

Are you ok?

ARAMINTA

Yeah, I'm fine. I could just use some water.

MAJOR

You and me both. I bet when the damn mayor privatized the water company, he never thought it would lead to a full-on rebellion.

ARAMINTA

Do you have any?

MAJOR

We only have a little water left, and I have the inmates on strict rations. I may be able to get you some later. In the meantime, have this.

(MAJOR hands her a small orange. ARAMINTA stares at it in awe.)

ARAMINTA

Where'd you get this?

MAJOR

You're not the only one with secrets. Stop asking questions and eat it.

(ARAMINTA unpeels and savors the orange throughout)

ARAMINTA

They said we couldn't survive without running water, but 3 years later—we still here. Still standing.

MAJOR

Are you really ok? When I heard they blocked all of the roads and were shooting everyone who tried to pass, I just thought the worst…Na nga def? (Wolof for "How are you?")

ARAMINTA

Mangi fii rek. (Wolof for "I am here only.")

MAJOR

Alhamdulillah. (Arabic for "All praise is due to God alone.")

ARAMINTA

That's good, Major!

MAJOR

Yeah?

ARAMINTA

Yeah. From what I've seen, the spies don't even remember our languages exist. Keep learning. It will keep you safe once we're outside of these walls.

MAJOR

Tell me—what's it really like out there?

(ARAMINTA slips into a trance. It's as if she can see into the before and the after.)

ARAMINTA

America's rotten roots are showing
Her roots blanched with greed
Poisoned with blood
Diseased from the start
Babies are starving in the streets

while the wealthy feast off the toil of all of us.
The ground beneath us will not hold
as the veils of truth are snatched back.
The people are rising up everywhere and this time we win.

(The lights flicker and blackout for a moment. They struggle to power back on after a few moments.)

ARAMINTA

(Snapping out of her trance)

What was that?

MAJOR

We are low on power. The backup generators kicked in but I'm pretty sure they'll be down soon.

(MAJOR observes ARAMINTA who doesn't seem to be all together well.)

I see you're still having your spells. Do you want to sit down?

ARAMINTA

I can't sit. I have work to do.

MAJOR

What work?

ARAMINTA

We've gotta get these people out of here.

MAJOR

What people?

ARAMINTA

Everybody locked up in here.

(MAJOR's whole demeanor changes.)

MAJOR

You mean my prisoners?

ARAMINTA

Yes, Major. I am here for everyone you call a "prisoner."

MAJOR

Have you lost your mind? I fought tooth and nail to gain control of this place. You know how hard I worked to earn respect from damn near everybody in here and I'm running things now. I'm one of the only ones left.

ARAMINTA

Major, listen to me—the people locked up behind these walls deserve freedom just as much as anybody.

MAJOR

Deserve freedom?! Do you have any idea the shit I faced for being who I am? Most of these folks need to be behind bars and you know it!

ARAMINTA

You know better than that, Major! Most of these folks are here because they were addicted, didn't have citizenship paperwork, needed mental health support, or because our damn city criminalized homelessness.

The vast majority of these people are ONLY here because they can't make bail. They're stuck in this cage only because they can't afford the price of freedom. That's it! "These people"—they are OUR people. They are US.

Their only real "crime" is being poor. Or Being Black. Being Brown. Indigenous…And even for the actual "criminals" we know this system is a failure. It was never meant to heal anyone—it was built to lock up Black and Brown bodies and use us as slaves.

MAJOR

Say what you want, but I'm not letting these people out.

ARAMINTA

If they stay here, they will starve to death, Major! You have a chance to be their hero right now.

MAJOR

I'm already their hero! I went from inmate to admin! I made sure folks in here got better food, made sure we honored Amendment A after it passed. The folks working for the state behind bars now earn minimum wage. I created the first unit for trans people. I have done right by these inmates and you know that!

ARAMINTA

That's all good but you're not thinking! There is an uprising happening outside these walls, sis!

MAJOR

An "uprising"? Don't be dramatic. Whatever this is will end soon enough. They always do.

ARAMINTA

Not this time, Major. This is the one we've been waiting for. Just think. The Colorado sun burns at over 130 degrees during the day—what about the sick? Your doctors ran off—what's your plan when people start to die? You gonna have all these lives on your hands?

MAJOR

If it keeps just one person out there from having to face the attacks I dealt with in here—then yes!

ARAMINTA

Of the thousands of people in here, how many hurt you?

(MAJOR is silent.)

How many?!

MAJOR

When I was on the men's side, my whole block jumped me one night. The things they did to me—

ARAMINTA

Sister, I am so sorry they hurt you. But what kind of person would you be if you let thousands of people perish because of the actions of a few cruel men? That's our family behind these bars, Major. People who are experts in surviving under the worst conditions. We're going to need an army if we're going to make it through this thing and this place is full of warriors!

MAJOR

Hold on. You're talking about using a bunch of broke down inmates to overthrow the American government?! Mint—you are out of your damn mind.

ARAMINTA

Everybody here is ripe for a revolution—they know how to gather resources in an underground ecology and how to make moves quietly. And more importantly, they know how to take care of one another. They know how to love each other, how to support each other…

When I was locked up—the women on my block helped keep me sane. The wisdom in these walls is enough to change the course of history.

MAJOR

What about when the staff comes back, Mint? You think they're just gonna ignore my empty jail?

ARAMINTA

Think of every unnatural disaster around the country where inmates were left to fend for themselves—Katrina, Sandy, Michael. They left our people in cages with no access to food, water or even ventilation. Children in raw sewage up to their chests. The government sentences our people to die every time. Nobody came back for us then; nobody is coming back for us now.

MAJOR

But what is your plan, Minty? You can't just start releasing people and handing out guns without a real strategy!

ARAMINTA

Who said anything about guns?

(She pulls a dandelion out of her pocket.)
We will give people this to keep them safe.

MAJOR
Ooh, sweetie—you've really lost your mind. That's a weed, Minty. What's that supposed to do?
(ARAMINTA laughs.)

ARAMINTA
Do you know where I plucked this? Right outside that window. I started eating dandelion greens when I was locked up in this very cage. I was always getting sick, they never gave us vegetables, and one day I was reading this book
(She finds Emergent Strategy by adrienne maree brown on the library shelf.)
and I read: "a dandelion is a community of healers waiting to spread." Then I had a vision of my grandmother making these leaves into a tea. Turns out it is the most nutritious green in the world.

MAJOR
Oooook. But how is that gonna replace guns, Araminta?

ARAMINTA
The more I ate them, I started noticing changes in myself and right before I was released, I started waking up outside my cell.

MAJOR
You're dehydrated, Minty! A damn weed can't do that!

ARAMINTA
Yes, it can. How you think I got past the guards, Major? This is it.

MAJOR
A dandelion?!

ARAMINTA
The dandelions here are special. I tried regular ones while I was

out and none of the flowers in the free world worked. I guess the dandelion transformed the high concentration of toxins in the jail soil…into magic.

MAJOR

If this jail had a yard full of magic, these white folks would've swooped down and took that shit by now.

ARAMINTA

They have no idea. The very poison they tried to use to destroy these dandelions made them into our weapon. Did you know the more you try to get rid of a dandelion, the deeper its roots shoot down into the earth? That when you break one down—all of those little puffy pieces fly away, plant their seeds and multiply? They are unstoppable and they will keep us alive.

MAJOR

I don't believe you, Mint.

ARAMINTA

Eat this.

(She hands her a small piece of the puff.)

MAJOR

I'm not eating that!

ARAMINTA

Your life depends on it! Eat it!

(MAJOR reluctantly takes it and nibbles a small corner. As she eats the dandelion, the power shorts out and we are plunged into Blackness. When the lights come back up, MAJOR has disappeared. ARAMINTA sits alone in the jail library. A knock at the door. ARAMINTA goes to answer it.)

ARAMINTA

Password?

MAJOR

(From outside the door)

Girl, I don't have time for no damn password! Let me in the fucking room, Mint!

(ARAMINTA opens the door as MAJOR bursts into the room.)

MAJOR

What kind of witchcraft is that?! One minute I was here—then I felt more awake than I've ever felt in my life. The next thing I knew—I was on the other side of the door.

ARAMINTA

The more you take, the further you travel. We need to start everyone on a diet of them today. We will be ready to travel by the end of the week.

MAJOR

We've been talking about liberation for years and you never mentioned this?

ARAMINTA

I didn't want to put you in danger with your new position AND I needed time to figure out the plan.

MAJOR

And this is what you came up with? This is your plan? Give a bunch of raggedy ass plants to a jail full of criminals and teleport them where, Mint? The whole damn country is on fire. Where are you going to take these people and how are you gonna be sure they don't kill anybody when they get there?

ARAMINTA

For the past two days, I visited with the elders of the Lakota nation. They will give us sanctuary on their land north of here and will heal all of us traumatized by this place. I left a bunch of the seeds with them and they have already started cultivating them.

MAJOR

This is insane, Minty!

ARAMINTA

There are over 40,000 people in Colorado cages—jails, prisons, so-called immigrant "detention" centers. Over 2.7 million people caged in the country. The U.S. military only has 1.7 million fighters left. If I harvest the dandelions here, if I travel to each prison and every jail and free their people before it's too late—we will win this war.

MAJOR

But how can we be sure this is going to work?!

ARAMINTA

Why did you name yourself after Miss Major Griffin-Gracy? Why?

MAJOR

I took her name because I hope to fight as hard for my people as she fights for hers.

ARAMINTA

If you truly mean that, then this is your moment to show up. Otherwise, you're not worthy of her name.

MAJOR

Damn, you act like I haven't been working for the people from day one! From every protest we went to, to getting arrested with you, to beating the cases and getting the charges dropped—everything I've done has been for the cause of Liberation.

ARAMINTA

That's right. And you always said you wanted to be in power for this very moment. What did Ms. Hamer say?

MAJOR

"Nobody is free until everybody is free."

(She thinks and then finally)

Those men from my old block have to stay. They're being held in solitary and they will remain there.

ARAMINTA

But they can be healed too.

MAJOR

No. I will die before I fight alongside them.

ARAMINTA

Ok.

(This is hard for her but she knows it's the only way MAJOR will concede.)

They will stay.

MAJOR

You will make the announcement over the loudspeaker first.

(She hands ARAMINTA the mic.)

ARAMINTA

(ARAMINTA hands the mic back.)

You make the announcement. They need to hear from you.

MAJOR

(MAJOR stares at the mic for a moment. Gathers her resolve, turns it on and begins to slip into her own kind of trance.)

Attention, everyone under the sound of my voice. This is your comrade, Major. I want you to listen to me close, ok? Society has said you were worthy of being thrown away. Forgotten. Said you were worthless like those weeds that grow out on the yard. But my sister Minty here just reminded me that everybody listening to me is made of pure magic. It's time for us to harness our power, heal and fight back. Do you understand me? From this moment forth you are free. Once your cages open—if you want to band together, join us in the yard. If you want to go—feel free to do that too. The choice is yours. May justice come swiftly for us and ours. Fight with us!

MAJOR AND MINTY

Fight with us! Fight with us!

(Thunder claps. Lights flash bright then BLACKOUT.)

END.

Note: This is an adapted version of the play that was originally performed in *Bite Size: An Evening of Micro Theatre.*

HOLY COUCH

by Edith Weiss

CHARACTERS:

JIM: Late thirties to early sixties, white collar. Typical hard-working white collar man.

JUDY: His wife, late thirties to early sixties, a woman aging attractively.

PLACE: A couch in a living room.

PLAYWRIGHT'S NOTE: In the script, Jesus refers to the Son of God. *Jesus* is the Spanish pronunciation, and refers to the Mexican gardener.

AT RISE:

(A living room, couch center. Window Stage R, light streams in. Sound of a game, football or hockey. Sound of a leaf blower OFF. Enter JIM, who turns up the volume, then crosses to couch, as he begins to sit down he stops.)

JIM

Holy shit.

(Looks closer)

Oh my god. Judy! Judy, come here!

JUDY

(From off)

What is it?

JIM

Come into the living room!

JUDY

Can't it wait? I just—

(Sound of leaf blower stops)

JIM

No! No, it can't wait. Jesus is on the couch!

JUDY

Honey, it's pronounced *Hesus*. And what is he doing on the couch? Is the leaf blower broken?

JIM

It's not *Jesus* the gardener! Just get in here, will you?

(JIM turns off the T.V. JUDY enters. She has just put a mask on her face, and has been painting her toenails; she has cotton between her toes.)

JUDY

What is going on, Jim? I'm trying to get ready—

JIM

Judy, look. It's Christ's face, on our couch.

JUDY

Oh, come on—oh my god. It does look like Jesus.

JIM

I told you. Thorns and everything.

JUDY

It's just a trick of the light. Look, the sunlight is streaming in—

JIM

The sunlight has streamed in every day for the fourteen years we've lived here. Has it ever looked like this?

JUDY

No.

JIM

No.

JUDY

It looks like his eyes are looking up, like in the paintings.

JIM

It does.

JUDY

I'm scared, Jim.

JIM

Scared?

JUDY

What's he doing here? Why is Jesus on my couch?

JIM

It's got to be a sign.

JUDY

Of what?

JIM

I don't know.

JUDY

If he's trying to tell us something, why doesn't he just say it?

JIM

Don't get defensive.

JUDY

I'm not defensive, I—I guess I'm flabbergasted. No one's ever going to believe this.

JIM

They're going to think we're crazy.

JUDY

Take a picture. Let's see if it comes out.

JIM

What, if it doesn't come out, Jesus is a vampire?

JUDY

This is no joking matter, Jim.

(They take a selfie with Jesus.)

There he is. Clear as a bell. Let's send it to someone and see if they see it.

(We hear a lawn mower. The sound can increase and decrease as the yard is mowed.)

JIM

They're just going to think we photoshopped it.

JUDY

Right. So. What should we do?

JIM

I don't know.

JUDY

Maybe we should pray to it.

JIM

Oh, I don't know.

JUDY

What? We go to church.

JIM

Twice a year, not counting weddings and funerals.

JUDY

Stop with the jokes. This is serious. We pray in church, so why not here? Jesus is right here, so let's pray. Come on. Get on your knees.

(Both kneel. Silence.)

Are you praying?

JIM

Yes.

JUDY

What kind of a prayer?

JIM

I don't know. Just a prayer.

JUDY

Well what are you saying?

JIM

It's private.

JUDY

Jim! I don't think it should be private, and I don't think it should be just a prayer. We're in this together; he's in our house. On our couch. So why don't we pray together, out loud? You first.

JIM

Out loud?

JUDY

Are you ashamed?

JIM

No! Of course not. It just feels…weird.

JUDY

Just say something to Jesus from your heart.

JIM

Our Father, Who Art in Heaven, hallowed be thy—

JUDY

Jim! Jesus is not Our Father; God is our Father.

JIM

Are you arguing theology now?

JUDY

No. I'm sorry. It's just that I was brought up Catholic, and there's the Father, Son, and Holy Ghost. They're the same, but not. So, I think we should specifically pray to Jesus, the Son.

JIM

Okay.

JUDY

And I think it should be an original prayer, from the heart. He's right here. He can hear us.

JIM

He can always hear us!

JUDY

I know that! But He's on our couch! So I think it should be more personal. All right? Okay. So let's talk to Him. Go ahead.

JIM

I haven't prayed out loud since I was six.

JUDY

Open your heart, honey. He's right here. He likes that.

(Pause. JIM clearly doesn't know what to say. Lawnmower sound stops.)

JIM

Hi Jesus. Uh…you wanna beer?

JUDY

Jim! That is not funny! Why can't you take this seriously?

JIM

Hey, why wouldn't Jesus want a beer? He changed water to wine. So you know booze was all right with him.

JUDY

Jesus is not a frat boy! I'll go first. Jesus, please forgive Jim. He's just nervous. But You know he loves You. So do I. We love You very, very much. And…we want to thank You. Thank You for our blessed life. The kids, the house, the food; thank you for Jim's job…

JIM

…The QLED T.V.

JUDY

Jim!

JIM

I love watching sports on it. And I'm thankful for it.

JUDY

It's trivial!

JIM

Not to me—

JUDY

We're in the middle of a very profound experience—

JIM

You know what's trivial? My job! Writing commercials for pharmaceuticals!

JUDY

That's not trivial. You're fighting disease.

JIM

Right. Viagra and Botox fight disease.

JUDY

They make people feel good about themselves!

JIM

And that's what Jesus wants? For us to feel good about ourselves?

JUDY

I think so.

(JIM scoffs)

What's wrong with that? You can't love others if you don't love yourself!

JIM

"Cause I'm worth it," right?

JUDY

What is wrong with you? That job got us this house! It's putting our kids through college.

JIM

So they can get better jobs, make more money, and watch bigger T.V.'s.

JUDY

I don't like this. What is the matter with you?

JIM

Jesus is on our couch!

JUDY

Which should be a good and blessed thing! Right?

JIM

I guess.

JUDY

But why? Why is Jesus on our couch?

JIM

And God said, "Let there be light." And there was light. God saw that the light was good, and He separated the light from the darkness.

JUDY

That's from the Bible, isn't it?

JIM

Yup. Genesis. Third verse.

JUDY

I forgot you knew the Bible.

JIM

Baptist born and raised.

JUDY

So what do you think it means, the face of Jesus on our couch?

JIM

I don't know.

JUDY

We're good people. Maybe He's here because we're good people.

JIM

Yeah. Sure.

JUDY

We are good people!

JIM

Good people? I work all week writing persuasive bullshit, very subtly planting fear—you're old—nobody loves you—you smell—nobody loves you—you can't get it up—nobody loves you—and on Saturday, I spend the entire day on the couch, watching my giant T.V.

(Starts to sit on the couch, close to where Jesus is.)

JUDY

Don't sit on Jesus!

JIM

(Bounding off couch, recovers)

Or I play golf. What is good about that?

JUDY

We are good people. We don't hurt anybody, we work hard, we pay *Jesus* more than the neighbors do—

JIM

Ah, yes. *Jesus*. Comes here every week, keeps the lawn green, trims the hedges. And we can't even talk to him. And you know what? We like it that way. That way, we don't have to say what we both suspect; he's an illegal alien—

JUDY

—undocumented worker.

JIM

—undocumented worker. We don't want to know, because he's cheap. And if he gets thrown out of the country, that's okay too, he's just the yard boy. There's plenty more where he came from. So really, either way, our asses are covered.

JUDY

This isn't about *Jesus*.

JIM

Judy—if Jesus' face is on one's couch, and *Jesus* the Mexican gardener is spreading weed killer in one's backyard, couldn't that be more than just coincidence?

JUDY

You're scaring me.

JIM

What doesn't scare you, Judy?

JUDY

You know what doesn't scare me? That sarcastic, condescending tone of yours—that doesn't scare me. So, Mr. High and Fuckin' Mighty, what do you suggest we do now? Turn *Jesus* in? Throw a quilt over Jesus on the couch? What?

JIM

I'm sorry, Judy. I didn't mean to talk to you like that.

JUDY

I know, honey. It's okay. We're both upset. And I'm sorry, Jesus, swearing in front of You like that. I'm going to do a rosary tonight, I really am. For penance.

JIM

You have a rosary?

JUDY

Yes. I'm sure it's around here somewhere. God, my mask is starting to itch. Jeez, what a stupid thing to say in front of the Son of God! He's on a cross, dying for the sins of all mankind, and I'm complaining about my mask starting to itch!

JIM

And we were fighting, too. We have a rule about not fighting in front of guests.

JUDY

This is so unnerving.

(Kneels again. Speaks sincerely)

Jesus, we want to do things the right way. But things have gotten so complicated in this world. Even while I thanked you, for all the good things you've given us, I felt guilty. I feel guilty all the time, Jesus. All the time.

JIM

You do?

JUDY

Yes! How can you not? We have so much. We have too much. So much food I have to drive to the gym to walk the treadmill for an hour—cause I eat too much and I don't want to get fat—and then people will shame me and nobody will love me. You've given us so much. Or, we've taken it, I don't know. I don't know what to do, do we give it all away? Become poor and meek and powerless? Please, tell us what to do.

JIM

Give it all away? Are you serious?

JUDY

Didn't Jesus give it all away? Didn't he tell his Disciples to? Didn't He say something about a rich man getting into heaven was as likely as a camel trying to thread a needle?

JIM

(Searching for Bible from the shelf)

Well, not exactly. Where is that Bible? Here. It's uh—Matthew—Matthew 19:23. Here it is. "Again I tell you, it is easier for a camel to go through the eye of a needle than for someone who is rich to enter the kingdom of God."

JUDY

There it is.

(Grabs lamp, remote, phone from end table)

We are giving all of this to charity.

JIM

Are you crazy? We can't just give everything away. We've worked our whole lives—Judy?

(Gently taking things from JUDY)

I would still love you if you were fat.

JUDY

Really, Jim? We're talking in front of Jesus, so don't lie—give me your best honest answer—would you love me if I were fat? Really, really fat?

JIM

I would love you…but…maybe a little differently. I mean, you wouldn't be the same, would you? But no—of course I would love you, just the same—I mean, say you gained the weight really slowly, and I really didn't notice—

JUDY

And then one day, I'm 550 pounds—

JIM

I would love you. I would love that…that would be great. Would you love me? If I were really, really, fat, and couldn't play golf, could barely walk, and didn't have enough breath to make love to you?

JUDY

(Pause)

I don't know. I really don't know. I mean, I'd love you, but I don't know if I could…God, this sucks.

(We hear the SOUND of a trimmer)

JIM

We could change, Judy. We could become worthwhile, I mean, in Jesus' eyes—we could strive to be meaningful.

JUDY

We could make a difference. Oh, Jim, we could. Let's pray about it.

(THEY both kneel)

Jesus, thank You for coming into our home. Thank You for showing us the light—

(THEY look at Jesus' face. The light from the window dims.)

JIM

He's fading.

(Sound of trimmer stops)

JUDY

He's gone. Where did he go?

JIM

(Walking to window)

There's a cloud in front of the sun. That's all. He'll be back.

JUDY

Oh, yes, I want Him to come back. We have to tell Him. He's changed our lives.

JIM

It's a big cloud. It could take a while.

(JUDY kneels in thought for a while. Then:)

JUDY

This mask is so itchy. I'm going to go and wash it off. I won't be a minute.

JIM

Okay. I'll be right here.

(JUDY exits. JIM waits a while, looking out the window, and down at the couch. Then, JIM picks up the remote, turns on the T.V. We hear the sounds of a sport being played. JIM slowly sits on the couch, carefully avoiding the spot where Jesus was, watching the game, reacts to the game:)

We need a miracle here!

END.

MARGINALIA

by Jeffrey Neuman

CHARACTERS:

J: The manager of a used bookstore

M: A customer

PLAYWRIGHT'S NOTE: M. and J. can be cast by actors of any race, ethnicity, gender, physicality, and sexual orientation/ identity. The actors must, however, give a sense that these two characters are somehow cut from the same tentative, introverted, and somewhat lonely cloth.

For ease of reading I've designated M. as female and J. as male.

SETTING: A used bookstore with a smattering of tables and chairs, some of which look more used than the books.

SYNOPSIS: A bibliophile is confronted by the manager of a used bookstore when she is caught defacing some of his product.

NOTE ON PACING AND FORMAT: I encourage the actors to have fun finding, embracing, and playing with silences and awkward pauses. This short piece is about two human beings who are hungry to connect, but uncomfortable and a bit uncoordinated in doing so. Take your time; the play should feel more Vladimir and Estragon than Abbott and Costello.

Also, please note that dashes and ellipses do not have to be played exactly as written in the script; they are simply suggestive of the halting and highly navigated quality of the exchange between these two characters.

M. is sitting at a table reading, chewing the end of a ballpoint pen or absently running the end of the pen against her teeth. There is a small stack of closed books on the table in front of her, an assortment of titles, both fiction and non. At rise, she is reading a novel, perhaps a classic, perhaps a bestseller, perhaps something obscure. Whatever it is, she is thoroughly engrossed.

A moment later, J. walks by the table, simply doing one of the many daily tasks of bookselling (re-shelving a book, for example, or picking up books left at another table). He exits as M. continues to read. A long silent beat.

Eventually, J. passes by again, just as routinely, though he does mumble an "Excuse me" as he picks up a crumpled piece of paper (a receipt? a tissue?) From the floor next to M.'s chair. She takes note of him, somewhat, but quickly returns to her reading. He exits. Another beat.

M. turns the page of her book, but then…there's something about the passage she's just read that makes her turn back. She reads it again and…nods, very subtly, to herself. The nod turns into a surreptitious glance to her right and then to her left. Confident she's alone, she uncaps her pen and underlines several sentences in the book; she then begins to write something in the margin next to this highlighted passage.

In the throes of documenting her thought, M. doesn't notice J. re-enter. (Nor does she notice how he stops when he takes note of what she is doing.)

J.

Excuse me, but, um…you can't…y'know…

(He sort of gestures at the book. A beat.)

…You're going to have to buy that.

M.

Oh. Okay.

(He eventually nods, the issue seemingly settled. He turns to continue his work, but as he does:)

Why?

J.

Because. It's not yours.

M.

Yeah, but…it's used. All of them are.

(Her gesture suggests more than just the books in front of her, but rather the entire store.)

J.

…That doesn't mean that you can…use them…more.

(She nods in what seems like acceptance of this statement, but then:)

M.

Isn't that why you sell them, though? Used books. So that they can be…used. More.

J.

Yeah, but…you have to *buy* them first, before you…y'know.

M.

Oh. Okay.

(Once again, there is a sense that the conversation is over, that a matter settled, when he turns to leave, though:)

Why?

J.

Because. You just…do.

(She nods. A heavy beat as he looks at her, yet she cannot meet his gaze. Eventually:)

M.

But, if I buy them,

bring them home,
read them …
And, I write in them there, just …
jot a few notes in the margins …
(She lets the thought hang for a beat)
I can bring them back, right? Resell them. That's what you do?

J.

…In theory.

M.

In theory?

J.

Yes. You can bring them back.

M.

So, why can't I just write in them here? Now?

J.

Because…that's just not the way it works. You have to buy them. And, you *can* write in them, but…you can't—y'know—they need to be…resellable if you bring them back.

(She nods. He nods. It seems an understanding has been reached. Having been stopped in his tracks the past few times when he thought the conversation was over, though, he stays this time. Waits it out. A long tug-of-war beat. He turns to leave:)

M.

Do you ever read them?

J.

The books?

M.

(She shakes her head)
What people have written in them.

J.

(He shrugs)

I guess. Sometimes.

M.

I always do.
I think it's…fascinating. To see what passages or words or… turns of phrase they've underlined,
what…made them…
Take notice.
The things they've decided need to be…held and…
…considered. Y'know.
To see what…ideas or information or…sentiments have spoken to them, so much so that they need to be marked.
For revisitation.
It's like the perfect snapshot of a person and a thought and…a moment in time.
Don't you think?

(He doesn't answer, not only because the question feels rhetorical, but also because he doesn't quite know how to answer. A short beat, before M. launches into a story that feels like a jumping in, of sorts, a trust fall.)

M. (CONTINUED)

Once—I came across this book of poetry in a dollar bin by the front door of a used bookstore. It was a really skinny little book called *The Country Between Us*. Isn't that a lovely title? The Country Between Us. Well, when I opened the book, I was just …amazed at how much had been written in it. Just note after note on page after page, these…recorded thoughts *right there*, so that they could live with the poems, interact with them, become part of them. Become…part of the book itself. What I noticed most, though, was on one of the pages…
…a water spot.
Tiny.
Maybe the size of a pea, right on the edge of the page, right next to one of the poems. And, the reader had circled the water spot with blue ink and written the words "My Tear" next to it.
I read the poem, which was nice, but not particularly tear-worthy,

in my opinion. And, I wondered…why did it make her cry? What about the poem or its message affected her so deeply? Maybe it wasn't even the poem. Maybe she was just depressed, maybe it was just a bad day, maybe she just felt hopeless and alone, for whatever reason a person feels…hopeless. And, alone.

(A long, awkward beat, that neither M. nor J. know how to fill, though J., for whatever reason, feels onus to be the one who breaks that silence. Eventually:)

J.

A few years ago, this guy brought in a boxful of books. He didn't want any money for them, just…to be rid of them, I guess. They were old. Mostly trash. Probably a—dead relative's or something. I was sorting through them, trying to figure out what to keep, what to toss, and, um, there was this one old, old textbook in there about human sexuality and, um, intimacy. It must've been, like, one of the first books ever published on the subject. I mean…real old school. Literally. Well, I was flipping through it, because, y'know, why not, and there was this whole chapter on the…"causes" of homosexuality. And, someone'd written in the margins: "My mother made me a lesbian." Underneath that—someone else had written…"If I buy her the yarn, will she make me one, too?"

(Slowly and surprisingly, they both begin to laugh. It is not bellyache or showy laughter, but rather soft and genuine.)

One of the funniest things I'd ever seen.

M.

That *is* funny. And, extraordinary, when you think about it:

Two people who'd never met, having an exchange that they'd never share, all in…a way that may never be witnessed.

I guess that's why I always make a point to read them. The notes in books.

(They continue to share the receding waves of laughter. Eventually:)

J.

Why do you do it, though? I mean, I kinda get why you like reading what's written in them, but…why do you do it yourself?

Write in them.

(M.'s laughter and smile fall away; she could answer this question in so many different ways, but...any answer she can think to give just seems too intimate. Too vulnerable. A beat. An adjustment. She holds his gaze for as long as she can before breaking and looking down at the stack of books on the table. The moment of conviviality has ended and they, rather abruptly, find themselves back in a place of supreme awkwardness.)

M.

Do I have to buy all of them?

J.

Um, well…how many did you, y'know…?

M.

Just…a couple.

(Her look moves, very surreptitiously, from the books on the table to the stacks of books surrounding them. He sees and understands that her writing is probably peppered throughout many, many of the books in his store. He sighs.)

J.

…Pay for whatever you can—today.

(M. nods, before picking up the last book that she'd written in, opening its front cover, and looking at the price scrawled in pencil on the title page.)

M.

You write in them, too.

(She shows him.)

J.

That's just…the price.

(She nods again, looks at the price again, and nods yet one more time.)

M.

I…didn't bring my purse. Only enough for lunch. And the bus ride home.

(She reaches into her pocket, pulls out some money, more change than bills, and begins to count out the nominal fee for the book, which is perhaps $2.75. Eventually J. stops her:)

J.

Just…

(He doesn't have to say "take it," because his gesture, a gesture that may surprisingly be more exasperation than kindness, says it all.
It looks as though M. may say more, but she doesn't. She just collects herself, smiles at him, and begins to leave. She turns very suddenly before she exits.)

M.

Thank you.

(J. looks at her.)

Not just for this…

(Holding up the book he has given her)

…but for…

(She does something to suggest the shop as a whole and all of the books within it. A beat.)

There's nothing sadder in the world to me than a book that's gone untouched. Unread. Unmarked. I mean…what's a book without…a story?

(She nods. And, exits.)

(J. stands there for a moment, thinking about the exchange. He walks the short distance to M's table and is about to pick up and reshelve the books she's left there. He puts his hand on the cover of the topmost book. It is clear he wants to open the book to assess how much she has written in it. It is unclear if he will do so, though, or if he will read what she has written, as lights fade to black.)

END.

OUTSIDE THE ROOM

by Theater Artibus, Grapefruit Lab + Larry Mitchell

PLAYWRIGHT'S NOTE: GREGOR will be represented by shadows played under the table and against the tablecloth at selected points by either MOTHER, FATHER, or SISTER.

ACT I

Scene 1: Morning

(A Parlor. A TABLE. Four CHAIRS.)
(SISTER is sweeping/dancing, and is interrupted by MOTHER and FATHER.)
(MOTHER and FATHER sit at the table.)

SISTER

One morning, as Gregor Shackleton awoke from his anxious dreams, he discovered that he had been changed.
Into a monstrous, verminous, bug.

(SISTER begins establishing THE RITUAL with MOTHER and FATHER.)
(THE RITUAL establishes the family's relationship to one another, place, and the expectations for the day. SISTER sets the table for four after bringing FATHER his paper. MOTHER watches with an eye for detail. Once FATHER AND MOTHER are cared for, SISTER joins them at the table, and they begin to eat.)
(Where is GREGOR?)
(The ritual is interrupted by a loud SCRATCH and HISS.)
(After a shared moment of hesitance and recognition, THEY begin to investigate via the KNOCKING CYCLE: ALL trying their own approaches to see if GREGOR is in the room or get him to come out.)
(At some point, SISTER peeps through the keyhole:)
(SHADOW: Image of keyhole)
(SHADOW: As SISTER looks through keyhole, it widens to reveal a cockroach.)
(She turns to share a "look of horror" with MOTHER and FATHER.)
(SISTER jumps on FATHER to get off table swiftly.)
(THEY share a look of horror. SISTER moves into the work of cleaning up and re-setting for the ritual.)
(Perhaps a gesture or physical sequence that establishes the passing of time.)

Scene 2: Proper Care and Feeding

(FATHER and MOTHER have returned to their seats. The ritual restarts, but nobody wants to eat. ALL three are staring at the door. MOTHER begins sobbing. FATHER consoles her.)
(SISTER, uninterested in sitting with this moment, combines the rubbish onto a plate, approaches the door, knocks...)
(Scurrying...)
(MOTHER faints. FATHER shrugs to SISTER, moves to help MOTHER.)
(SISTER opens the door, reaches the plate through, and dumps it, before pulling back out and shutting the door.)
(SHADOW: Door opening)
(SHADOW: Hand dumping plate)
(SHADOW: Door closing)
(Scurrying...)
(SISTER watches through the keyhole as GREGOR eats the food)
(FATHER and MOTHER return to their seats, looking to SISTER for information or explanation, but SISTER just returns to the ritual and resets.)

Scene 3: Business As…

(ALL run through the ritual, which now includes eating and then feeding GREGOR)
(SHADOW: Door opening)
(SHADOW: Plate dumping food)
(SHADOW: Door closing)
(There is a growing lack of care about the situation and the ritual. Just going through the motions...)
(This builds to ridiculous heights, as the PARENTS move into handing SISTER dishes as soon as she can dump them.)

Scene 4: The Last Straw

(SISTER can no longer keep pace with the MOTHER and FATHER's expectations and slams the plates down.)
(Everything stops.)

SISTER

It must be gotten rid of.

(SISTER moves to the broom, picks it up, and menacingly returns to the door.)
(SISTER walks through the door for the first time, eyes GREGOR, and delivers a very deliberate death blow.)
(SISTER sweeps GREGOR under the table, out of sight beneath the tablecloth with the help of MOTHER and FATHER.)
(ALL return to the ritual.)
(During the prayer, ALL discover that SISTER now has an insect-like appendage.)
(MOTHER and FATHER retreat immediately, grabbing the broom on the way out, turning out the lights, and shutting the door behind them.)

END.

PLAYWRIGHTS' NOTE: Our production and process were unique in that a good deal of the narrative was created and evolved in concert with the ensemble. Below you will find how the ensemble turned the preceding prompts that they collectively created into a list of actions for use in production.

Episode 1—Establishing Ritual/Establishing Absence

SISTER—light and gesture

SISTER dance/sweeps—perhaps voiceover here

PARENTS—light/gesture—interrupt SISTER dancing

Get objects for table

MOTHER pulls out chair for FATHER

SISTER sets table

MOTHER gets paper

MOTHER teaches SISTER how to place silverware—a shared process

Exchange tray and silverware

Sit and ALL scoot in

MOTHER time moment—where is he?

FATHER gets up, maybe, to acknowledge his absence

Ritual happens—end is a roll-off of the larger gestures

SISTER clears silverware and plates
Goes for GREGOR's plate

MOTHER gets FATHER's attention

ALL converge on chair and step in
Look at chair, look up at door

Moment of confusion/weaving—SISTER puts tray away

MOTHER knocks—strict/annoyed

Cue up by rotating SL to SR

FATHER goes next—slurp sound

ALL jump back

FATHER gets off the table scared (maybe he jumps into MOTHER'S arms)

FATHER and MOTHER cross slow/menacing SL to SR to pressure SISTER

SISTER goes to door and knocks

FATHER comes up to cover as MOTHER goes under table

SISTER looks into keyhole momentarily and sees just a leg—big gasp and scared/surprised reaction

SISTER looks longer—long cockroach viewing—responds with disgust
Grossed out movements—over FATHER'S shoulder

MOTHER faints, FATHER tries to revive

SISTER begins the weaving, PARENTS join

Return to places—begin new episode/new ritual—lights on/off

Episode 2—Loss is Acknowledged and Felt

SISTER sweep/dances

Lights/gestures—Parents interrupt

MOTHER gives whole tray to SISTER and sits

SISTER sets table

MOTHER gives FATHER paper

Begin ritual—food sniffed in disdain, mother cries on prayer

Ritual happens up until moment of biting food—ALL give up on food

SISTER—collect silverware and scrapes all plates onto GREGOR'S plate

SISTER gets on table—MOTHER closes the gap—FATHER sneaks under

SISTER opens door and gives food in a sweet way—closes door—resets plate

FATHER back to paper—MOTHER cries on table

SISTER returns to sweeping

Episode 3—Sister Picks up the Slack/Parents Return to Normal

FATHER demands food prompting MOTHER to demand place settings

SISTER puts broom away

MOTHER (SL) with plates and FATHER (SR) with silverware—hand off items to SISTER

PARENTS sit expectantly at table, waiting to be served

SISTER does plate and silverware setting ritual

SISTER goes to sit, FATHER stops SISTER from sitting

MOTHER, FATHER, SISTER weave in and out, taking turns in the middle

FATHER passes GREGOR'S plate down—SISTER grieves it

FATHER passes silverware down—SISTER gets rid of it

They remove GREGOR'S chair

They ALL sit

ALL begin ritual (starting with scraping of silverware, followed by four points on plate)

SISTER gets up and dumps her own plate more carelessly—not finishing the ritual

We see the dumping part in SHADOW
SISTER comes down

MOTHER collects plates and gives to SISTER

<u>Episode 4—Parents Continue Demands/Feeding Never Stops</u>

SISTER sets the three plates (starting SL)

SISTER does not sit to eat but takes her plate immediately up to door and throws the contents into the room as the PARENTS begin the ritual

SISTER comes down

PARENTS shove plates back at SISTER (in rotation style)—with SISTER resetting right from her spot (SR)

SISTER gets onto chair—pushes door open and dumps from chair—gets on table

Food dumping ritual with PARENTS passing plates in rotation—plates just appear nonstop—SISTER starts standing and ends squatting—crescendo

SISTER slams plates down—SISTER is done—"It must be gotten rid of"—(*Spoken*)

Episode 5—Getting Rid of Gregor

SISTER gets broom—resolute

SISTER makes decision to kill him and does

SISTER sweeps under table—MOTHER assists with tablecloth

SISTER gets rid of broom and sits

Ritual begins again

SISTER'S cockroach arm is revealed

MOTHER & FATHER gather broom and exit to outside…the room…

END.

TOXOPLASMOSIS

by Sean Michael Cummings

DRAMATIS PERSONAE:

ALI: Male, 22, "Black"

HANNAH: Female, 35, "White"

VETERINARY ASSISTANT/BEAR: "Whatever"

PLAYWRIGHT'S NOTES:
/ Indicates the point where the next line should start
— Indicates an interruption
...Indicates a short pause

NIGHTMARE MODE: Ignore the grammar and use your judgment.

Berenstain is pronounced "Beren-STAIN."
Berenstein is pronounced "Beren-STEEN."
"Hypmosis" is pronounced like "hypnosis," but with an "m."

SETTING: A veterinarian waiting room equipped with chairs and a coffee table festooned with light reading.

(ALI sits, hands lightly bandaged, reading The Berenstain Bears' Trouble With Pets. *HANNAH enters and plops down on a chair across from ALI. After a pause, she notices ALI's book.)*

HANNAH

(Pointing)

Hey.

(He ignores her.)

Dude. Dude. Dude. You wanna see something funny?

(ALI looks up, annoyed. HANNAH pulls a book out of her purse: The Berenstein Bears' Trouble With Pets.*)*

ALI

Ah. Very nice.

HANNAH

(Dancing the book around:)

Book twins.

ALI

Yeah. "No spoilers."

HANNAH

Oh they're pretty formulaic so you can't actually—

(Off his look:)

Oh! Haha! / Pretty funny.

ALI

Thanks—thank you.

(He resumes reading. She puts her copy back in her bag. A pause.)

HANNAH

Do you have an early reader?

ALI

'Scuse me?

HANNAH

A child? You have a child you read with?

ALI

I'm, like, twenty.

(Beat.)

HANNAH

Plenty of people have kids at twenty.

ALI

…I know.

HANNAH

I had a kid at twenty.

(Small pause)

ALI

Well you absolutely cannot tell.

HANNAH

But can you call him an early reader? An autistic teenager? That's like the opposite of an early reader.

ALI

I really wouldn't know.

(He reads.)

HANNAH

So what, you just "like-a da Bears?"

(He doesn't respond.)

…just a Big Stan and Jan fan?

(He doesn't respond.)

…Stan and Jan Berenstein?

ALI

I find them overly moralistic.

HANNAH

Oh.

ALI

(*Low:*) And I think it's "Berenstain."

HANNAH

What?

ALI

Uh. "Berenstain," I think it's pronounced.

HANNAH

What?

ALI

...Never mind.

HANNAH

"Berenstain?"

ALI

"Berenstain," yes.

HANNAH

What is *that*?

ALI

Their name.

(She scoffs.)

Check.

HANNAH

I don't have to. I've read them many, *many* times with my son.

HANNAH	ALI
They are, and always have been, The Berenstein Bears—	Well I read them with my mom but—

ALI

Stain.

HANNAH

By Stan and Jan Berenstein—

ALI

Stain.

HANNAH

Proud Jews.

(Beat.)

ALI

Maybe you should check.

(HANNAH produces her phone.)

HANNAH

(Mispronouncing "meme") No thanks. I will not be taking part. This is some kind of internet mémé or something.

ALI

(*Quiet*)…It's "meme."

HANNAH

Hm?

ALI

I didn't say anything.

(HANNAH texts. ALI resumes his book. He finishes it. He checks his watch, and claws at one cheek with a groan.)

(He scans the room. His gaze falls on an imaginary waiting room T.V. He winces.)

ALI

(*Mostly to himself*) Why does Animal Planet have a dog abuse show?

(HANNAH watches the screen. ALI disengages. A pause.)

HANNAH

It's a dog rescue show.

ALI

Uh what.

HANNAH

It's a rescue show; they rescue the dogs. From like drug dealers.

ALI

"Drug dealers."

HANNAH

It's a good—it's uplifting.

(Beat.)

ALI

(*Pointing*)…This is the bleeding, caged dog you're looking at.

HANNAH

Yes.

ALI

…is "uplifting"

(Beat. Enter VETERINARY ASSISTANT, in lab coat or scrubs, with clipboard and a small white cardboard box.)

VETERINARY ASSISTANT

Sorry about that wait, guys.

HANNAH

(*Chipper:*) No problem.

VETERINARY ASSISTANT

Which one is "Spooky"? Owner of "Spooky."

HANNAH

Right here.

ALI

That'd be me.

(A pause.)

VETERINARY ASSISTANT

Ah, oops.

(Flipping pages:)

I mean Spooky the, uh, black…female cat.

HANNAH

I'm here.

ALI

Yeah.

VETERINARY ASSISTANT

(Flipping pages:)

…Black female cat…between …five and six years.

HANNAH

Yes.

ALI

That's my cat.

VETERINARY ASSISTANT

Um. I'll cut to the—which of you two wanted the funeral package?

(Beat. ALI and HANNAH stare at VETERINARY ASSISTANT aghast.)

VETERINARY ASSISTANT (CONTINUED)

(*Slightly alarmed:*) W—OK. Let's take like eight giant steps back.

You. Sir. Your cat's named Spooky?

ALI

Yes.

VETERINARY ASSISTANT

And you, Ma'am…

HANNAH

Yes?

VETERINARY ASSISTANT

…you also own a cat?

HANNAH

Yes.

VETERINARY ASSISTANT

Also named Spooky.

HANNAH

Spooky, that's correct.

VETERINARY ASSISTANT

So…whose Spooky was supposed to be euthanized and cremated?

(A pause. The VA shakes the box promptingly. We hear ashes inside. Another pause.)

<table>
<tr><td>HANNAH</td><td>ALI</td></tr>
<tr><td>My Spooky tangled
her tongue in a string.</td><td>Mine had the…
sudden aggression.</td></tr>
</table>

(Beat. VA flips clipboard pages.)

VETERINARY ASSISTANT

(*Muttering:*) Oh man. Uh…the printer?

(To HANNAH and ALI, with growing panic:)

Sorry guys, today has been—we had an unexpected large-animal case this afternoon and it put us a few pets behind schedule and everyone is a bit, you know: Chickens with our Heads Cut Off. Which, normally, we'd sew those bad boys right back on! Ha ha! Just a bit of veterinary humor but that's not really possible in actual p—WOULD YOU EXCUSE ME??

(VA hurries off with the box. HANNAH and ALI sit, stunned.)

<table>
<tr><td>HANNAH</td><td>ALI</td></tr>
<tr><td>Oh my God. My son
loves that cat.</td><td>Whoa, Spooky?</td></tr>
</table>

(HANNAH pulls out her phone to write a Yelp. ALI idles to the VA door.)

HANNAH	ALI
(*A dark invocation*): One fucking star.	Hey I'll just take Spooky now. burnt, unburnt, I'm probably just…
One fucking star.	
	…gonna go.
One fucking star. (*typing MADLY*)	
	You have any condition cat back there?
One-fucking-star.	
	Or like a coke machine? Cause I've been waiting here for like…
Yelp death… to this Evil Backwater	You can hear me.
ROBBER	
Strip mall veterinarian who killed	
	(*Loudly:*) What kind of large animal do you have back there, a panda?
MY CAAAAAAAAAAAAAAAT.	

(HANNAH throws her phone. They both watch it clatter across the room.)
(A pause.)

ALI

Yours or mine?

HANNAH

What?

ALI

Your cat or mine? They never said.

(Beat.)

HANNAH

Oh my god I have no idea.

ALI

Right.

HANNAH

I'm gonna cry. I'm gonna, actually, throw up and cry.

ALI

(Pointing, dryly:)

Trash can.

HANNAH

I wasn't even there to cradle her little head. You know, in the event that it…
I DON'T KNOW WHETHER TO MOURN MY KITTY / OR

ALI

Ah. It's a Schroedinger's Cat.

(Short beat.)

HANNAH

Come again!?

ALI

It's kind of…a Schroedinger's Cat?
The metaphysics one where you box / up the cat and —

HANNAH

God; Millennials.

ALI

What?

HANNAH

You're all so…?

ALI

What?

HANNAH

Your cat just got murdered; you're like making references.

ALI

May have got murdered.

HANNAH

"May have," whatever.

ALI

Metaphysically.

(Beat.)

HANNAH

This is real life.

(ALI nods. A pause.)

HANNAH

So do you just not care for this cat? Or —

ALI

She's my mom's. Ok? If you must know. I'm taking care of my Mom's cat.

HANNAH

Oh. So is Mom…?

ALI

(*An unclear euphemism:*) She relocated to Florida.

HANNAH

Uh.

ALI

(Inward, getting his story straight:)

Relocated to Florida.

(Beat. He displays his bandages:)

And Spooky's psychotic about it, so I came here, so she'd stop mauling me. Which…I guess, in a way, panned out.

HANNAH

Shouldn't you call her?

ALI

Who?

HANNAH

Your mom?

ALI

What??

HANNAH

In Florida.

ALI

Oh.

HANNAH

I'd just want to know if my cat was…maybe, metaphysically, dead.

(HANNAH's discarded phone rings. She stomps over to it, checks the caller, closes her eyes, and sighs deeply.)
(She answers.)

HANNAH (CONTINUED)

Mom. Hi. Is Danny OK?

(Weary:)

The Vet Hospital. Spooks? Remember?

(Beat.)

Yeah. There ya go. Uh, not too good actually. Spooky's—at least, presumed to be…uh

(Beat.)

No, I'm not sure. I'll update you I guess.

(Beat.)

What did you just see on YouTube.

(Beat. HANNAH heaves a sigh.)

HANNAH

(Quoting her mother's mispronouniation:)

"Hypmosis." Ok, Mom—"Brain parasites."

(Beat.)

Mom? Mother? You don't—you don't even touch the litter box. OK? Neither does Danny. So it isn't brain worms or whatever you're implying and—

No, I don't want any of your theories on my son anymore.

HANNAH (CONT'D)

Because—look—maybe—maybe CAT SHIT ISN'T TO BLAME, Mom, maybe there's NO BLAME. Maybe there's just autism, and, and incompetent medicine, and death, and maybe it's time we stopped trying to paper over that fact with science-fiction internet BULLSHIT! OK??? And I'm hanging up now because you're making me swear in public!

(HANNAH hangs up. She grabs the trash can and heaves once into it, but nothing comes up. She puts the trash can aside. A pause.)

HANNAH

Moms.

(HANNAH rubs her temples. A pause. ALI clears his throat.)

ALI

You wanna see something funny?

(HANNAH smiles wanly. ALI grabs The Berenstain Bears' Trouble With Pets *book from the table.)*

ALI

So. It actually is "Berenstain." As I was saying before. But—

HANNAH

God save us from men in 2018.

ALI

Hah?

HANNAH

Who told you this?

ALI

(Mild offense:)
It's on the cover.

HANNAH

No. The cover says —

ALI

THIS IS WHAT I AM SAYING. LISTEN TO ME. I thought that too. But it's wrong. It's—you ever—you know subreddits?
NOPE.
OK you know the Mandela Effect?

HANNAH

The band?

ALI

No. Remember when Nelson Mandela died in prison? Like 1983 or 4?

HANNAH

Yes.

ALI

Right. But you don't. Because he was released from jail in 1990 and died in 2013 at age 95.

HANNAH

…and thank God for that.
(Beat.)

ALI

…yeah. But a lot of people think like you do. So the Mandela Effect says that either this widespread memory of Mandela's 80's death are wrong—or:
(With great mystery:)
We're remembering traces of an alternate dimensional timeline intertwining with our own.
(Beat. HANNAH snorts and commences rifling through her bag.)

ALI

What.

HANNAH

(Rifling:)

Why are you all so obsessed with multiple dimensions?

ALI

What do you mean "you all?"

(Ignoring this, she produces her copy of The Berenstein Bears' Trouble With Pets *[with alternate spelling].)*

HANNAH

(*Comparing the copies*) And why's my copy say "Berenstein" then?

(Beat.)

ALI

What?

HANNAH

(Pointing to cover) "Ber - en - stein."

(She frisbees it to him. ALI now has the Berenstein *book, and HANNAH the* Berenstain *book.)*

ALI

(Looking the Berenstein *book over:*) Is this a joke?

HANNAH

Is *this* a joke?

ALI

Uh. Read that title. Of the book you're holding. Right now.

HANNAH

The Berenstain Bears' Trouble With Pets.

ALI

The Berenstain Bears' Trouble With Pets! Right! We're the

"Stain" Universe! So where'd this come from??

HANNAH

…the ARC?

ALI

"The ARC."

HANNAH

Scholastic book drive maybe?

ALI

NOT POSSIBLE!

HANNAH

Whoa.

ALI

Sorry. Sorry. Uh—look, what's your name?

HANNAH

Hannah.

ALI

Hannah. This whole thing—my mom read these to me a lot when I was younger? And when she went—uh, moved. To Florida. Like, the day we put her in the…plane, this "Berenstain-not-Berenstein" thing hit, and I was like, losing Mom AND the memories, in this weird way, like,

(Trailing off:)

It made me go a little like, borderline, uhh…

(A pause. He flips through the pages of the Berenstein *book.)*

HANNAH

It's ok.

ALI

I'm much better now.

(Flipping pages, low and intense:)
"Berenstein." Every time.

HANNAH

Look…uh?

ALI

Ali.

HANNAH

Ali. Look, truly, I'm sure it's a typo, or —

ALI

No. No. You know what this is Hannah?

HANNAH

A galley proof?

ALI

This: is nonexistent.
(Beat.)

HANNAH

I'm sure there's a rational—

ALI

I don't think so. No. Something is happening. First the cats. Now the books. This is all VERY—what we're experiencing is a phenomenon called "High Strangeness."
(Beat.)
Something is coming.

HANNAH

What is "coming."

ALI

(Getting excited now)
No idea. No idea. Something big. A visitation.
(A pause in which nothing happens.)

HANNAH

Well how 'bout a visitation from that vet assistant, eh?

ALI

What if we touched them together?

HANNAH

I'm sorry?

ALI

What if we touched. The books. Together.

HANNAH

I mean…what if I say "Beetlejuice" three times.

(ALI stomps over and grabs the Berenstein *book. He takes it in one hand and the* Berenstain *book in the other.)*

(With great ceremony, he brings the books together.)

(Nothing happens.)

(He brings them together several more times.)

ALI

Oh. *(he tosses the books on the coffee table, mortified.)*
Uh. OK. Uh. Sorry; that was…sometimes I still get a little, uh, my meds are still…

(He trails off. A beat.)

HANNAH

You're good.

ALI

(Meaning his mother)

I think I miss her?

HANNAH

Yeah.

(Beat.)

(The door opens)

HANNAH

Well hey. At least it looks like we can get some—OH MY GOD!

(A BEAR, played by the same actor as the VA, staggers in. Its head is wrapped with bloody gauze.)

ALI

OH SHIT!

(THE BEAR roars. It really takes a lot out of him.)

HANNAH	ALI
MAKE YOURSELF BIG! MAKE YOURSELF BIG!	BEAR! BEAR ON THE LOOSE IN HERE!

(THE BEAR looks at ALI. It looks at HANNAH. It staggers over to the coffee table to catch its breath.)

HANNAH

It's not showing a lot of hustle.

(THE BEAR picks up the Berenstein *book and replaces it with a slim white paperback. It looks from ALI to HANNAH. It removes its bandages and drops them on the floor. It makes a "shushing" gesture at them, followed by a throat-slitting gesture.)*

(BEAR exits. A pause. HANNAH points at the bandages on the floor.)

HANNAH

Did those just come from / a bear…?

ALI

A bear. It was a bear.

HANNAH

Thank god. I thought I stroked out.

(Beat.)

This veterinarian is a fucking shambles.

(ALI crosses to the table and picks up the white paperback.)

HANNAH

Which did he take? The magic special-vowel one?

ALI

Yeah. The Berenstein.

HANNAH

Sorry Dude. Ali. Sorry Ali. What'd he drop off?

ALI

Uh…*Eat Pray Love.*

HANNAH

"Prey" with an E?

(With a little predator mime:)

Like, "prey"?

ALI

Just regular *Eat Pray Love*.

(Half a beat.)

HANNAH

(Encouragingly:)

Well that's pretty strange!

(ALI slumps in his chair, dejected.)

HANNAH

And a good read.

(Beat.)

ALI

I'm sorry I allowed a bear to steal your son's book.

HANNAH

No! No.

ALI

If your Spooky's dead, you can have mine if you want.

HANNAH

I'm probably good.

ALI

Yeah. She's aggro.

(HANNAH nods. A pause.)

HANNAH

You OK?

ALI

I just thought like…The Path Would Reveal Itself. I thought that book was like …a way out.

HANNAH

Every book is a way out.

(A beat. ALI makes a face. The VA re-enters carrying two cat carriers.)

VETERINARY ASSISTANT

Hey kids! Sorry again about that *un*acceptable wait.

You guys are not going to believe this: we actually admitted THREE cats named Spooky today! So BOTH your cats are both fine! Plus they're on some pretty good meds. Sir, this one's yours and—wait.

(VETERINARY ASSISTANT swaps the carriers.)

VETERINARY ASSISTANT (CONT'D)

Sir, this one's yours, and here's yours, ma'am. Come get your babies!

(HANNAH and ALI uneasily collect their pets.)

VETERINARY ASSISTANT

(Seeing the bandages on the floor:)

Whoa. Are those—did a bear come through here?

(HANNAH and ALI say nothing.)

VETERINARY ASSISTANT

It's up to me now.

(VA shoulders a tranquilizer rifle.)

Linda will settle up with you down the hall.

(Exit VA, pursuing BEAR.)

ALI

(Showing his bandages:)
But the aggression —?
(Beat. Meaning the VA:)
They're gone.
(Small pause)
OK. Well. Hannah. This was memorable.

HANNAH

You too Ali.

ALI

Maybe I'll see you over at Linda.
(He starts off.)

HANNAH

Hey, do you—?

ALI

What?

HANNAH

Uh—this is gonna sound stupid maybe—but, I dunno, do you wanna…be read to? For a bit?
(Picking up the Berenstain *book:)*
Berenstain Bears?

ALI

I just finished that.

HANNAH

Oh.
…*Eat Pray Love*?
(A pause.)

ALI

…I mean, sure.
(They sit awkwardly with their cat carriers.)

HANNAH

OK. Comfy? Alright, um. *Eat Pray Love.* By Elizabeth Gilbert. Chapter one. "I wish Giovanni would kiss me. Oh, but there are so many reasons this would be a terrible idea. To begin with,

Giovanni is ten years younger than I am, / and —"

ALI

I gotta go.

(ALI exits.)

HANNAH

OK.

(HANNAH sits alone for a long moment.)

HANNAH

(Muttered) Beetlejuice, beetlejuice —

(Her phone rings. She pauses.)

(She places the book on the coffee table, takes her cat carrier, and exits with ringing phone.)

END.

SOMETHING TO READ AT THE END OF THE WORLD

by Maureen Biermann

CHARACTERS:

BOOKSELLER: A man in his fifties

YOUNG WOMAN: A transgender woman in her late teens or early twenties

PLAYWRIGHT'S NOTE: Stories about transgender individuals are still relatively rare in theatre and film. Transgender actors are currently almost never cast to play cisgender roles, whereas cisgender actors are frequently cast to play transgender roles. Because of this imbalance of opportunity, and because of the urgency and importance of recognizing and validating the existence of transgender people in our society, the granting of permission to perform this play is dependent upon the casting of a transgender actor in the role of Young Woman.

SCENE: A secondhand bookstore in a city not too far from here.

TIME: A quarter to six in the evening, on a day in the not-too-distant future.

AT RISE: We are in a secondhand bookstore in a city not too far from here, in the not-too-distant future. It is evening, around a quarter to six. A large sign in the window reads: "FREE BOOKS." The BOOKSELLER, a man in his fifties, is perusing a bookshelf marked "Rare and Collectibles." He periodically takes a book down and examines it, sometimes putting it back, sometimes putting it in a large cardboard box that is already almost full of books. A bell rings as the door opens and a YOUNG WOMAN enters. She is in her late teens or early twenties and looks a little wary. She is transgender. The BOOKSELLER looks up as she enters.

BOOKSELLER

Looking for something to read at the end of the world?

YOUNG WOMAN

The sign says you got books for free?

BOOKSELLER

All of them. Take whatever you want, except what's in the box.

(YOUNG WOMAN begins to browse.)

YOUNG WOMAN

(Gesturing toward the sign in the window)

No "Liquidation Sale" like everybody else?

BOOKSELLER

I like a good pun, but that feels a little too morbid to me. Anyway, they're not for sale, they're free.

YOUNG WOMAN

Hard times bring out generous spirits.

BOOKSELLER

I'm not generous. Nobody's going to buy them. No room in their luggage. And most everyone has left by now anyway. I might as well give them away.

YOUNG WOMAN

Aren't you going to try to come back for them later?

BOOKSELLER

Nah, books don't survive a flood.

YOUNG WOMAN

If you stacked them all up on the top of the shelves, maybe the water won't—

BOOKSELLER

They'll mildew from the humidity even if they don't get wet.

YOUNG WOMAN

Oh. That's sad.

BOOKSELLER

Yup. Yeah. It is. So I'm rescuing what I can. My car is mostly full up, but I've got room for one more box, and about—

(Checking his watch)

— fifteen minutes to fill it.

YOUNG WOMAN

You leave at six? You got stuck with a late evacuation slot.

BOOKSELLER

More time to pack up.

YOUNG WOMAN

Less room for error.

BOOKSELLER

Well at least it's not the last slot. Hopefully the roads aren't bad. No accidents, last I checked the traffic report. The evac system is actually working like it is supposed to. You at 6 pm too? Or did you get stuck with 6:30? You should still be okay, they said the water won't start to rise till late tonight. It takes that long to make its way down from the mountains.

YOUNG WOMAN

I don't have an evac slot.

BOOKSELLER

You're taking one of the shuttles to the shelter at the Arena? Huh, I thought they all left already.

YOUNG WOMAN

(Gesturing to the box of books)

How do you decide which ones to rescue?

BOOKSELLER

It's…not easy. I've owned this place for twenty years, and collected a lot over the years. Even though I buy them to sell them again, a lot of them hang around for a long time in between. You appreciate them in the meantime. You start to get attached. And the group of them that stick around for a while, it starts to feel like…I don't know, like they belong together or something. Or maybe more like somehow when you put all of these random books together, you get something special that emerges. Put together they make up something bigger than each of them by themselves. Which they do, I guess, they make up the shop, the…placiness of it. This place is the place it is because of them. It changes a little when one book comes and another goes, and it has evolved over time, but it is what it is because of the books.

(He sighs.)

It hurts to leave. It hurts to leave them behind. I wish I could save them all. But I can't. So how do I decide which ones to rescue? Do I take the rarest books? Do I take my personal favorites? Do I take the ones that are worth the most?

YOUNG WOMAN

You should take the smallest books, so that you can rescue the greatest number of them. Maximize quantity, since you can't rescue them all.

BOOKSELLER

(Chuckling)

The utilitarian approach! I like it! But is that looking at too broad of a scale? Maybe I should focus on rescuing the greatest number of words, and select the books with the smallest font.

YOUNG WOMAN

(Joining in the joke)

That's ableist. Large print books for the visually impaired don't stand a chance.

BOOKSELLER

What would you take first?

YOUNG WOMAN

Duh, the most valuable. The ones you can resell.

BOOKSELLER

A-ha! But those aren't the same thing.

(Passing her a book)

Should I take this one?

YOUNG WOMAN

Analytical Drawings of Australian Mosses?

BOOKSELLER

It's worth around a thousand dollars. It's somewhat rare, and old, and decent condition.

YOUNG WOMAN

Seriously? Who would pay a grand for this?

BOOKSELLER

Exactly. You see my dilemma. It requires a very specific type of customer. It's been hanging around on my shelf for years waiting for the right buyer. I'm not sure I can afford to take it with me to hang around on the shelf, or more likely in a box somewhere, for another decade.

YOUNG WOMAN

(Handing the book back to the BOOKSELLER)

So it gets left behind to molder. Or drown.

BOOKSELLER

Sadly. But, yes.

(The BOOKSELLER goes to replace the book on the middle of the bookshelf, but stops himself and places it on top of the highest shelf instead.)

YOUNG WOMAN

So…instead, you take the ones that are worth a bit and that somebody wants now, not in ten years.

BOOKSELLER

(Nodding)

First editions, early printings, signed things by popular authors, the like. And a handful of rare and precious things will come with me, just because I can't bear to think there will be one less of their kind in the world.

YOUNG WOMAN

May I?

(The YOUNG WOMAN gestures toward the box. The BOOKSELLER hesitates, then nods. The YOUNG WOMAN begins looking through the books in the box and reading the titles.)

Good choices. *To Kill a Mockingbird, The Picture of Dorian Gray*—

BOOKSELLER

Both later editions, but signed.

YOUNG WOMAN

Impressive. Hey, this one isn't even a book, it's a pamphlet.

(She holds up a small orange book and begins flipping through its pages.)

BOOKSELLER

Be careful with that! Very, very, very, very careful. That is a 1928 edition of W.H. Auden's *Poems*. Very scarce. It's the first thing he ever published. Published, actually, by his friend Stephen Spender, who was also a poet. He only printed a small batch. You can see where that one is numbered, facing the dedication: "No. 3 of About 45 Copies." In reality, he only ended up printing about thirty copies, and only thirteen of those are known to exist today.

YOUNG WOMAN

There's scribbling in it. Someone, like, corrected the text. Crossed things out and changed the words all throughout.

BOOKSELLER

Auden was a perfectionist, and didn't want to stop editing his work just because it went to printing. So he kept working on his poems and then later he and Spender went through each copy and put in the edits by hand. There's a famous quote by the French poet Valéry—"a poem is never finished, only abandoned." Auden's response to that was "yes, but it must not be abandoned too soon."

YOUNG WOMAN

(Reading from the book)

"Cocks crew, and sleeping men turned over./Rain fell for miles; ghosts went away./The jaw, long dropped, stopped at reply."

(The YOUNG WOMAN closes the book and looks at it for a moment, before placing it gently back in the box and taking out another book.)

Well I have to say this next one is a little unexpected. *The DaVinci Code*? I mean it was a fun read, but…

BOOKSELLER

A signed first, and I will admit it seems incongruous next to the Auden, but it'll get me some quick cash. Here's one you might like to take. Also a signed first, but not worth so much.

(The BOOKSELLER pulls a book from the shelf and hands it to the YOUNG WOMAN.)

YOUNG WOMAN

Margaret Atwood *The Year of the Flood*? Haha. Anyway already read it, and now I'm going to be living it. Don't want to read it again, thanks.

BOOKSELLER

Well what *are* you looking for?

YOUNG WOMAN

You nailed it, before. Something to read at the end of the world.

BOOKSELLER

A few good books for the road, eh?

YOUNG WOMAN

Nah, I'm stocking up. I'm not leaving. And I'm going to have time on my hands, so I need stuff to read.

BOOKSELLER

I realize this is none of my business, but…that's crazy. You know that, right? You'll die.

YOUNG WOMAN

Thank you for your input. So what books do you recommend?

BOOKSELLER

There is a reason they're evacuating. They're saying ten to twenty feet of water at peak. This whole place is going to be drowned. And they want to save the water because of the drought out west, so they're not planning to open the dam downvalley. Which means the water here isn't going to have anywhere to go. You'll be surrounded for weeks. Probably longer.

YOUNG WOMAN

Well then, now is your chance to answer the age-old, not-at-all hypothetical question: if you were stuck on a desert island and could take only one backpack full of books, what would you take?

BOOKSELLER

Stupid.

(Giving in, in spite of his frustration)

But, a first aid manual, a scouting guide for survival.

(He moves to the section labeled "Sports and Recreation" and pulls a couple of books off the shelf).

Let me think of what else. Are you sure about this?

YOUNG WOMAN

Yeah.

BOOKSELLER

A copy of *Walden* by Thoreau, maybe when you're feeling lonely, it'll help you remember other people have survived isolation. You religious? You want to take a Bible?

YOUNG WOMAN

No. Nope. I'll pass on that.

BOOKSELLER

Well then, poetry to nourish your soul, it is.

(He points the YOUNG WOMAN to the "Poetry" section.)

Rumi. Bukowski has some truly poignant, beautiful stuff even though he was a dick. Auden, of course.

YOUNG WOMAN

(Pulling books off the shelf)

Bummer, you're out of Auden. Do you have anything by Sylvia Plath?

BOOKSELLER

Too moody.

YOUNG WOMAN

No way. "Lady Lazarus" is my favorite poem.
"I am a smiling woman./I am only thirty./And like a cat I have nine times to die./This is Number Three./What a trash/To annihilate each decade."

BOOKSELLER

(Checking the shelf)

I'm out of Plath as well. But it doesn't matter because it sounds like you've got her memorized.

YOUNG WOMAN

My favorite ones, at least.

BOOKSELLER

What else? Fiction? Non-fiction? What do you like to read?

YOUNG WOMAN

Do you have *Hope in the Dark*?

BOOKSELLER

Rebecca Solnit? Here it is. That's a good one to read at the end of the world, because it'll leave you convinced that the world might not really be ending after all. *Parable of the Sower* and some LeGuin, and here's a good one that just came out a few years ago: Doctorow's *Walkaway*. Those will be fun for when you're ready to start thinking about what comes after the flood. With the flood and the drought and the riots on the coast, I'm not sure we're going to be able to go back to the way things were. It feels like things are changing.

YOUNG WOMAN

I know what you mean. It's hard to know where we'll end up.

BOOKSELLER

You know this is foolish. Actually, foolish doesn't even begin to capture the idiocy of your decision. You know that, right?

YOUNG WOMAN

I know you think you're right, but it's more dangerous for me out there than here, okay?

BOOKSELLER

I'm not sure what you think is going to happen out there, but there is *no place* that is going to be more dangerous than this place when the water starts to rise. Have you heard people talk about the floods of '65? Killed dozens of people, ruined everything, took years to rebuild. And this is supposed to be a lot worse.

YOUNG WOMAN

Trust me, I could be facing much worse. Where's your philosophy section?

BOOKSELLER

Over there.

What's worse than drowning? Or starving stuck on a rooftop somewhere for a week? Or shitting yourself to death because you don't have clean water?

YOUNG WOMAN

Hey, I found a sixth-floor apartment to squat in. I've got a water filter. A camp stove. Antibiotics. And a million freaking

Band-Aids. Yesterday, I found myself a blow-up raft and a life preserver. I've been collecting food and other stuff nonstop since the evacuation started. The rest of my building has been empty since this morning and I'm going to go home and scavenge whatever I can from the other apartments until the water gets here. I am set. I am fine. I just need something to read. This is my last stop and then I'm bunkering down in my cozy little disaster-proofed nest, safe and sound and ready for the water.

BOOKSELLER

I just don't get it.

YOUNG WOMAN

You don't have to.

BOOKSELLER

Look, there are places that'll take you if you don't have anywhere else to go. The Arena is set up for evacuees, there's food, beds, medical care. You'd be safe there.*(As he speaks, the YOUNG WOMAN pulls out her wallet and takes her ID out, and holds it up for the BOOKSELLER to see.)*

BOOKSELLER

What's this? Alan Marcus Reilly? This is you? So what. We're past that, nobody cares about that sort of thing any more.

YOUNG WOMAN

We're not past that. I'm not past that. That's the problem. It's not me. It was me, but that person is gone. It's not so easy to get identification for the me I am now. You need time and money and a court order from a judge and medical proof that you've had reassignment surgery and your new genitals match the M or the F you want on your ID. New driver's license, new social, new passport, new birth certificate, each has their own set of hoops to jump through and fees to get it done.

Moving about in the world without an ID, I mean a real ID that shows who I am, not who I was, is impossible. And dangerous.

BOOKSELLER

They don't care what your ID says at the Arena shelter. They'll let you in no matter what.

YOUNG WOMAN

They'll let me in, but it's not true that they don't care. My friend got there last night, he texted me pictures. They're checking IDs at the door. They're sweeping for immigrants, but they're saying it's to track who's there and to assign people to beds. If you're not with family, you're put into partitioned-off dorm set ups, one for men and one for women. They have men and women's bathrooms but the showers aren't private stalls, they're all open. What do you think will happen to me in a place like that?

I've heard stories from after the hurricanes, people like me being beaten up for using the men's room and beaten up and then arrested for using the women's. The same will happen to me, because I'm not a man, and even though I am a woman, there will be someone who looks at me and doesn't see a woman. Maybe if my ID was right, I could get put in the women's section and just keep my head down and make it through. It's harder to complain about me when I've got legal proof of who I am. But I know I'll go there and they'll take one look at me and one look at my ID and I'll be screwed from the get go. There will be zero chance I make it out in one piece. Truthfully, the ID probably wouldn't even save me, at best it would just buy me a little time. It's not safe there for people like me.

BOOKSELLER

I'm sorry. That's not fair. Sometimes I forget…It never occurred to me…

(He puts his hand on top of the full box of books, and checks his watch. He takes a long look at the books and spends a moment thinking hard, making a decision.)

"A poem is never finished, only abandoned."

(Speaking to the books)

Sorry for abandoning you, friends.

(Turning to the YOUNG WOMAN)

There's space for one more in my car. I don't have to take you to the Arena, I can take you wherever you want. I'm heading to my sister's up north, it's been drier there and it's safe from the storms and the flood. You'd be welcome there for a bit.

YOUNG WOMAN

You're inviting me to go with you? You said your car was full.

BOOKSELLER

I said there was room for one more box of books. But you could easily squeeze in instead.

YOUNG WOMAN

You'd do that? You'd leave the books behind so that I could come? You'd leave your Auden Number 3?

BOOKSELLER

Well, I'll find room for Auden, too, somewhere. Maybe in the glove compartment. But, yeah, I'm saying goodbye to the rest.

YOUNG WOMAN

That is…something. I mean, it's generous. Very generous. But I can't accept.

BOOKSELLER

Please don't be foolish. It is dangerous here. Please let me help you.

YOUNG WOMAN

I can't. I mean, I don't know you. You seem kind, you really do. You *seem* kind. But I don't know you. And I don't know where you're going, or where I'll end up if I go with you. Even if you really are the good person you seem to be, after you drop me off, wherever I end up next, with no ID, no job, no nothing…it won't be good.

BOOKSELLER

But don't you want to survive?

YOUNG WOMAN

Yes. That's all I want. That's what I've been trying to tell you.

BOOKSELLER

(Checking his watch)

It's six. I have to go. Close the door behind you when you leave, please, will you?

(He picks up the box of books and heads to the door.)

YOUNG WOMAN

Don't worry too much about me. I won't be alone, you know.

BOOKSELLER

You've got Rumi and Solnit and the rest to keep you company.

YOUNG WOMAN

Well, yeah, but I'm not talking about them. There are others like me. Afraid of violence, or immigration enforcement, or whatever other unimaginable threats that are out there. We'll stick together.

BOOKSELLER

(Picks up Auden's Poems *from the top of the box and holds it out to the YOUNG WOMAN)*

I really do think you'll need some Auden to read at the end of the world. Please take good care of Number 3.

(The YOUNG WOMAN takes the book.)

YOUNG WOMAN

"This is Number Three./What a trash, to annihilate each decade."

(BOOKSELLER leaves the shop with his box. The YOUNG WOMAN very carefully places Auden's Poems *in her backpack, along with the rest of her pile of books. She exits the bookshop, closing the door behind her.)*

END.

THE F WORD
A Play in Ten Minutes

by Claire Caviglia

CHARACTERS:

THE MAGICIAN: Male, late twenties to early thirties. The ringleader of the group.

MRS. MYRTLE: Female, past middle-aged. Retired middle school secretary.

MYSELF: Female, early twenties. The younger version of the fictional author.

PLAYWRIGHT'S NOTES: The audience participates in this piece as CHARACTERS, other thoughts of the fictional author.

SETTING: Inside the author's brain. The space is bare except for two chairs.

AT RISE: THE MAGICIAN stands on a chair, arms outstretched. MRS. MYRTLE sits on a chair near THE MAGICIAN, taking notes on a clipboard.

THE MAGICIAN

Ladies and gentlemen, boys and girls, youngsters and oldsters of all ages, welcome to the spectacular, death-defying, awe-inspiring…Monthly Meeting of the Mind!

(THE MAGICIAN encourages the CHARACTERS to clap.)

Wonderful, absolutely wonderful, most of you still have motor skills. I am, of course, your host, your entertainer for the evening, THE MAGICIAN!

(THE MAGICIAN encourages the CHARACTERS to clap again.)

And let's give it up for our Madame Secretary, Mrs. Myrtle!

(The CHARACTERS clap for a third time, while MRS. MYRTLE beams from her glasses.)

THE MAGICIAN

We are, of course, here to take attendance of which characters are still alive and kicking and haven't been…(*Whispers*) the F-word, and to vote on which character we will put to the forefront of our lovely author's brain! Any questions? No? Well, Mrs. Myrtle, let's start attendance!

(THE MAGICIAN approaches a CHARACTER/ audience member.)

Mr. Applebottom! Long time no see! How long has it been since our imaginative author worked on you…six months? Let's see… can you shake your head yes? Can you shake your head no? Can you speak? Yes! Wonderful! Glad to have you still with us. Mrs. Myrtle, mark Mr. Applebottom still here!

(MRS. MYRTLE does so. THE MAGICIAN approaches another CHARACTER/audience member.)

THE MAGICIAN (CONTINUED)

(*Flirty*) Jacquelyn Amber, how are you this evening? My, you look lovely today! I think it was just last week the author worked on you, yes? My, my, my, is that a new pair of earrings I see? I do love how descriptive she is. Mrs. Myrtle, account Jacquelyn Amber as alive and well and with a spiffy new pair of earrings!

(While MRS. MYRTLE attends her clipboard, THE MAGICIAN turns to face another CHARACTER. He has a grim look on his face.)

Oh…Griffenhopper. I see another sad, lonely month has gone by. Goodness gracious, the light has gone out of your eyes. Why, you can't even stand up! What happened to the rough and tough pirate that once roamed this brain, without a care in the world, a toothless smile on his face? Well, that's what sixty months of inactivity will do to you. Mrs. Myrtle, please mark Griffenhopper as…barely here.

(MRS. MYRTLE dutifully does so.)

THE MAGICIAN

Now, who do we have nex—

(MYSELF, an early twenties woman, enters from behind the CHARACTERS, carrying a book. She places the book in a vacant slot on the bookshelf.)

MYSELF

Um, excuse me? I'm looking for—well to be honest, I'm not quite sure what I'm looking for.

MRS. MYRTLE

Hello, dearie! You know, you look exactly like—

(THE MAGICIAN lets out a scream.)

THE MAGICIAN

SHE HAS SIGNED OUR DEATH WARRANTS!

MYSELF

Hi, um, sorry. I'm um…the Young Author. But, I go by Myself.

MRS. MYRTLE

You go by yourself where?

MYSELF

No, she calls me—well I mean, technically, I call me…she refers to me as "Myself."

THE MAGICIAN

Myself from twenty years and twenty pounds ago!

MRS. MYRTLE

Now, don't go getting upset. It's not like it's her fault—

THE MAGICIAN

It TECHNICALLY is!

MRS. MYRTLE

I'm Mrs. Myrtle, dearie. I'm based off your old elementary school secretary.

MYSELF

Mrs. Myrtle, that's right! Of course I remember you! You were so kind and could never say a bad word.

MRS. MYRTLE

Couldn't have said my character description better myself! (*Beat*) And this ball of delight, is—

(THE MAGICIAN stiffly holds out his hand.)

THE MAGICIAN

The Magician, at your service.

MYSELF

Wow, not even a first name.

THE MAGICIAN

It's part of my mystery!

MRS. MYRTLE

Do you know where you are, dearie? What you are?

THE MAGICIAN

Besides a giant pain-in-the-

MYSELF

Not really.

MRS. MYRTLE

Well, as a character in one of our author's books, a figment of her imagination, you are in her brain. You spent the first part of your time in the creative side of the brain, where she worked on you for—

MYSELF

Eight months.

THE MAGICIAN

Eight months?! She worked on you continuously for EIGHT MONTHS?!

MYSELF

She's working on an autobiographical one-woman-play—

THE MAGICIAN

A play?! A PLAY?! Our author is a novelist! A one-woman show! Do you hear that, Mrs. Myrtle?! Once that gets published, she'll start performing and never work on us again!

MRS. MYRTLE

The Magician's character description includes an overemotional disposition.

THE MAGICIAN

I beg to—

MRS. MYRTLE

And easily offended.

THE MAGICIAN

Take that back!

(MRS. MYRTLE ignores THE MAGICIAN. MYSELF surveys the room.)

MRS. MYRTLE

And now, since she is currently not working on you, you've traveled back. You've become a memory like the rest of us.

(She gestures toward the room)

Waiting to be finished so you can be transferred from the brain to living on the page.

MYSELF

So these are all the characters I've—she's written?

MRS. MYRTLE

Only the unfinished ones. Half-baked thoughts.

MYSELF

(Looking at the CHARACTERS)

Why are they sitting down? And not talking?

THE MAGICIAN

The dictator wants to know why her people suffer?

MRS. MYRTLE

Well you see, characters only progress as far as the author has developed them. For instance, take The Magician.

THE MAGICIAN

I am one of the most developed character she's ever written! Do you see the detail on these buttons? The inflection in my voice? My complex, dynamic attitude?

MYSELF

And overemotional—

THE MAGICIAN

The BEST most-compelling heroes have flaws!

MRS. MYRTLE

And I'm well-developed because I'm based off a real-life figure, easy to remember.

MYSELF

So I'm—

THE MAGICIAN

A threat to everyone you see here—

MYSELF

Probably the most well-developed character she has ever created.

THE MAGICIAN

Kiss-ass.

MYSELF

How can I kiss my own ass? Besides, maybe I haven't worked on you because you're so disagreeable!

THE MAGICIAN

Say that one more time, and I'll show you how I can saw a lady in half!

MRS. MYRTLE

Children, children, that's enough! We are here to work together.

THE MAGICIAN

Well I am! I'm not sure about her.

MYSELF

You can't fault me for just exist—

MRS. MYRTLE

We still have yet to get to new business! The Magician, I believe that's your cue.

THE MAGICIAN

(Straightening jacket)

Ah yes. New business. It would be my pleasure.

(THE MAGICIAN goes to stand on his chair while MRS. MYRTLE goes back to her chair.)

THE MAGICIAN

Everyone, everyone, can I have your attention, please? So sorry for that interruption! We are now going to move ahead to our new business: voting for the Character of the Month. Now, taking suggestions. Personally, I think Griffenhopper—

(THE MAGICIAN notices MYSELF'S raised hand.)

THE MAGICIAN

Yes?

MYSELF

Wait, you can control what the author writes about? Who I—she writes about?

THE MAGICIAN

(Snaps) You think these characters would be in this position if we could do that?

MRS. MYRTLE

Attitude, Mister!

(THE MAGICIAN takes a deep breath.)

THE MAGICIAN

No. We cannot directly control who the author writes about. But we can help align her thoughts, better our position, when she's not fully engaged. While she's sleeping for instance—

MYSELF

So that's how dreams work!

THE MAGICIAN

When she's driving or day-dreaming.

MRS. MYRTLE

It takes considerable energy to think thoughts that she has not. That's why we can only send one character.

THE MAGICIAN

Back to business—I really think Griffenhopper—

MYSELF

Wait, if I have the most energy here, why should I stay? I'm going to go fight for myself.

MRS. MYRTLE

We take turns, dearie.

MYSELF

You guys don't have to stay either. You still have energy. Go rally for yourselves. Don't be—

THE MAGICIAN

Don't say it.

MYSELF

Say what? F—

THE MAGICIAN

Do. Not. Say. It.

MYSELF

…Forgotten.

(MRS. MYRTLE cringes. THE MAGICIAN's demeanor changes. The pettiness falls away, and he stands straighter, adjusting his coat. His voice is calm and cold.)

THE MAGICIAN

You, mere girl, do not understand. You do not know what it's like to sit here: for weeks, for months, for years. Waiting desperately, for anything, to be worked on, to be completed, to for once in your existence feel whole. You see these characters, the ones that sit in silence, that only track you with their eyes? They were all once fully-functioning, three-dimensional characters like you and me. Characters with thoughts, feelings, personalities. It's not just about how well-developed she creates you, but that she continues to work on you until you're transferred to the page otherwise you are—you are—

(THE MAGICIAN'S voice breaks.)

I'm going to…I'm going to prepare for Griffenhopper's transport if there are no objections.

(THE MAGICIAN walks away from MRS. MYRTLE and MYSELF.)

MRS. MYRTLE

He had a wife. Her name was…well, I can't remember either now. He continued to grow, to be embellished, while she faded away. By the time the author came back to her, she was too far gone. So she removed her from the story entirely. And she was…

MYSELF

The F-word. *(Beat)* I'm sorry to hear that.

MRS. MYRTLE

It's happening more and more often. A few years ago our author got married and now has two young children. She hasn't had much time to write lately. So it's been harder for even our Characters of the Month to get worked on. She hasn't had the time.

MYSELF

I'm surprised…my life has turned out like that. I mean at this point, I'm writing so much. I never would abandon projects. And kids! *(Beat)* Who would've guessed.

MRS. MYRTLE

So you see why these meetings are so important.

MYSELF

I guess I should go apologize to him.

MRS. MYRTLE

You don't want to have a small space become even smaller. *(Beat)* You go, dearie. I'm just…I'm going to sit here for a few minutes longer. I've been feeling kind of light-headed lately.

MYSELF

Thanks, Mrs. Myrtle. You've always been good at giving advice.

MRS MYRTLE

Every moment is a teaching moment.

(MYSELF approaches THE MAGICIAN.)

MYSELF

I heard about your wife.

THE MAGICIAN

Desdemona. I called her Desi.

MYSELF

Glad she had a name.

(Her joke falls flat.)

Look…what I'm trying to say is. I'm sorry.

THE MAGICIAN

What does sorry do for me? For Desi? For them?

MYSELF

Look—

THE MAGICIAN

You've always been selfish, you know.

MYSELF

Can you just not accept an apology!? Not everything is an attack, okay? Why must you egg me, egg everyone on—I swear, we're fighting like brother and, and…oh.

THE MAGICIAN

(Pause)

Now you know why I'm still here. Why I'll always be here. Why I have to help everyone else.

(Beat)

Adam may be dead…

MYSELF

But his memory lives on.

THE MAGICIAN

(Beat) Just with a slightly fancier coat.

(A loud crash gets their attention. MRS. MYRTLE, clipboard and all, has fallen off her chair.)

MYSELF

Mrs. Myrtle are you—

(THE MAGICIAN pulls MYSELF back.)

THE MAGICIAN

Leave her be.

MYSELF

What? Why? Is she—is she being—

(A school-esque intercom blares, "Mrs. Myrtle to the principal's office.")

MRS. MYRTLE

It must be summer vacation. The school is so dark.

THE MAGICIAN

Oh no…

MRS. MYRTLE

What in…after all these years!

THE MAGICIAN

Mrs. Myrtle, the principal has summoned you!

MRS. MYRTLE

I can't go without saying goodbye to my kids!

(She walks toward MYSELF and THE MAGICIAN.)

It's been so good seeing you again, dearie.

(THE MAGICIAN kisses her hand.)

THE MAGICIAN

It's been an honor, Madame Secretary.

(She wraps THE MAGICIAN in a big bear hug and hands him her clipboard.)

MRS. MYRTLE

You take good care of that for me.

(To MYSELF)

You watch out for this one, he's nothing but trouble. In my office all the time.

MYSELF

Goodbye, Mrs. Myrtle.

MRS. MYRTLE

Better board the bus before it leaves.

(MRS. MYRTLE removes a book, her story, off the

shelf and leaves. THE MAGICIAN and MYSELF stand in silence, lost in contemplation.)

MYSELF

So that's it, huh? She's…gone?

THE MAGICIAN

If she were transferred to the page, she would have seen a light.

MYSELF

But how could I—she just forget?

THE MAGICIAN

(Bitterly)

Does our author even remember what she had for breakfast this morning?

(THE MAGICIAN gently hugs the clipboard and gingerly hands it to MYSELF. MYSELF takes the clipboard and goes and sits on MRS. MYRTLE'S seat. THE MAGICIAN returns to standing on his chair. He straightens his coat and outstretches his arms.)

THE MAGICIAN

Griffenhopper! Let's see if we can perform a disappearing act on you!

END.

THE MISSING PIECE
A Play in One Act

by Christina Miller + Addie Levinsky

CHARACTERS:

BUB: Male in his late sixties. He'd help a stranger change a tire. He shovels his elderly neighbor's sidewalk.

JOELLE: Woman in her mid-twenties. Her eyes smile at cashiers, even if her mouth doesn't.

LIBRARIAN: Librarian responsible for announcements.

SCENE: The puzzle table at the Downtown Denver Central Library at 7:50pm on a Tuesday in November 2018

SETTING: We are in the Denver Central Library on the main level, near the puzzle table. The library is about to close, so there is a buzzing atmosphere as people hurry to wrap-up emails, find books, and finish magazine articles. Homeless library patrons soak in one last bit of heat before heading into the chilly night.

AT RISE: JOELLE stands alone at the puzzle table, intently working the puzzle. She pauses periodically to scan the room. She listens to an audiobook wearing headphones attached to the phone in her back pocket.

LIBRARIAN

(Announced over intercom)

Denver Central Library will be closing in 10 minutes. Please proceed to Borrower Services or Self-Checkout.

BUB

(BUB with pursed grin raises a short wave and approaches JOELLE at the table)

JOELLE

(JOELLE acknowledges BUB, takes out her headphones and turns off the audiobook on her phone)

There's an edge piece missing.

BUB

Is there?

(BUB removes jacket and drops it to the floor while reviewing the puzzle)

Lots of progress since yesterday.

JOELLE

Yeah. All that's really left is all this damn brick and some of the blue doors. The doors are a bitch. They all look the same.

BUB

(BUB raises eyebrows questioning her aggression)

JOELLE

They do.

(JOELLE gesticulates frustration)

BUB

Just focus on the shapes.

JOELLE

I am.

BUB

How long has it been since you slept, kiddo?

JOELLE

Sorry…you know I haven't been sleeping, then I started binge listening to this book.

BUB

It must be good. Books usually put me right to sleep. What is it?

JOELLE

Infinite Jest. David Foster Wallace.

BUB

I've never heard of it. What's it about?

JOELLE

I'm at hour 34 of 56, and I'm still not sure I know. Tennis? Toxic waste motivated wheel-chair assassins? Addiction? Corporate consumption of the human soul? Deep self-loathing? And maybe, I don't know, mold?

BUB

Why don't you just pick up a John Grisham?

JOELLE

(JOELLE rolls her eyes)

And I'm also fairly certain that my mom knew this guy.

BUB

The author?

JOELLE

Yeah. I know a lot of people have huge vocabularies, but the words he repeats are so my mom. I even hear certain words in her voice: "prandial, supine, prone." But then also "diddle," and "dicky." Who talks like that, right? It's weird. And they're both obsessed with toenails, disease…deformities. Throw in addiction and schizophrenia—they're like two peas in a pod. And, no shit, my mom once told us that Vermont was infested with feral hamsters. She also told us to get the sleep out of our eyes or roaches would eat it and it would make us blind. Those two things are both in the book—just like she said.

(JOELLE pauses)

And, there is this fucked-up invalid rape scene where some asshole rapes his incoherent foster kid while forcing "it" to wear a Raquel Welch mask.

That's a

(JOELLE makes air quotes)

"your life is better than foster care" argument straight out of the mom's mouth. Now that I think of it, it's possible that she and David Foster Wallace fuck-maginated that scene together. It would explain a lot actually.

BUB

Whoa, kid. Sounds like the book's getting to you a bit, eh?

JOELLE

And the way he creates acronyms for everything—Jack does that. And there are so many characters like capillaries, all magically meeting at the heart. The guy is brilliant. And, he also writes about putting up an electric fence to keep out the mariachis.

BUB

Ooo. The edge piece has got to be here somewhere.

(BUB looks around table and grabs a different piece)

This one looks like part of a blue door with something red next to it.

(BUB looks calmingly toward JOELLE holding up the piece)

JOELLE

I hate mariachis.

(JOELLE looks at piece, takes it from his fingers and places it in puzzle)

Here!

BUB

You have her eye, that's for sure.

JOELLE

How's the misses doin' anyway?

(JOELLE scans room, then continues to work puzzle)

BUB

Well, yesterday she was telling me that she and her nurse served together in Korea. The nurse went along with it, which led to all kinds of nonsense. It was a good day. Then, she got on a singing jag…"Jesus Loves Me."

JOELLE

Aren't you Jewish?

BUB

Yes. She converted before we got married…since we'd planned to have kids.

JOELLE

Jesus *was* a Jew!

BUB

Helen still has a gorgeous voice.

(BUB switches spots with JOELLE and places several pieces he's put together into one of the blue door spots with a confident nod)

You know, we were talking about you and your brother, the other day, kiddo.

JOELLE

Yeah? What did she have to say?

BUB

She said she told your brother that if he didn't plant the bulbs in October, that he'd find himself in a mess of trouble.

JOELLE

Ha. She's making about as much sense as my book…and my brother.

BUB

I miss her. The old Helen, I mean.

JOELLE

I know, Bub. But don't forget the old things that make happiness possible.

(BUB nods)

JOELLE (CONTINUED)

Someone said that in the book. I didn't make it up. But I mean it…

(JOELLE nods and lets out a light sigh and points to piece she's just put into puzzle)

Does this fit?

BUB

(BUB adjusts glasses)

Um, yep. Looks good. It's hard to see in here.

JOELLE

You're old and it's late…you're usually here before me.

BUB

Today she wasn't so good. I had a hard time getting out.

JOELLE

Ughhh…what happened?

BUB

Seems she's convinced that I've sold the house out from under her. She kept screaming, "Give me the deed! Give me the deed, you dirty Jew!" Makes that whole episode from a few months ago where she accused me of stealing her panty hose seem pretty benign.

JOELLE

Damn.

(JOELLE scans the room, then returns focus to puzzle)

BUB

Yeah. Hey, thanks for listening, kiddo.

JOELLE

Anytime…

(BUB and JOELLE work puzzle in silence for about 5 seconds)

I'm looking for a brown one with two big tongues.

BUB

That's…what she said.

JOELLE

Oh my god, I wish I hadn't taught you that.

BUB

You know, sometimes edge pieces don't look like edge pieces.

JOELLE

Trust me, Bub. It's not here. I have the eye, remember?

BUB

Have you seen Jack today, kiddo?

JOELLE

No…but that guy he was with last week came in earlier. He told me that Jack stole his grounding stake and earthing sheet and that my bloodline is responsible for disrupting his natural electric state.

BUB

Translation?

JOELLE

Jack's still out there somewhere.

BUB

Alive is good.

JOELLE

Yeah.

(JOELLE scans the room and pauses)

JOELLE (CONTINUED)

I heard a kid OD'ed in the bathroom downstairs this morning. The security guard gave him NARCAN and they took him away.

BUB

Did he make it?

JOELLE

(JOELLE shrugs shoulders, scans room, returns attention to puzzle)

BUB

This library is becoming a day shelter. They were talking about it on the news last night.

JOELLE

Which is why Jack comes here, which is why I am here working on these bloody puzzles day after day. Today, I'm going to blame Jack's situation on the mom and David Foster Wallace, or should I say, dad?

BUB

Circumstances aren't ideal for either of us, kid; I'll give you that. But I have to say, I'm not so sure this book you're listening to is doing you any favors. Seems like it's hit a nerve.

JOELLE

More like a vein. I don't even really give a shit about the story. I can guarantee you it's a movie you'd walk out of going, "What the fuck was that all about?" It's just the way he strings words together; I don't know what else to say. I'm listening at 1.0.

BUB

1.0 from a 1.5 gal? OK. Just get it over and done with. Then get yourself an Erma Bombeck and laugh a little.

JOELLE

Oh, and I can't believe I didn't tell you this. There is a character named Joelle who was the most beautiful girl in the world, before she got acid thrown in her face. That's more than just a coincidence, right? It's not like it's a common name.

BUB

Ha. Like I said, Joelle, Erma Bombeck.

JOELLE

(JOELLE rolls eyes, puts in another piece, then scans the room)

That snow globe puzzle was much more satisfying. And it had all its pieces.

BUB

Helen loved that one. She collected them you know, snow globes.

JOELLE

Hey, Bub, I asked at the desk about the next puzzle and they said this is the last one in Helen's collection. Are you sure that's right?

BUB

It was. It is.

JOELLE

I'm surprised she'd put it back in the box with a piece missing. Not a single stray in the others. Between her anti-Semitic bullshit and the missing piece, she's kind of pissing me off today.

BUB

Huh, yeah. Well, the missing piece is on me I guess. She never got to finish this one…seems like everything went to shit so fast…One morning, I found her staring at her puzzle curio cabinet crying. In the end, she just asked me to take them away, so I chucked the pieces of this one in the box and brought all 167 boxes, minus a piece, I guess, down here. It took so many trips to carry them in; I had to feed the meter twice.

JOELLE

Well, that's true love. I think Helen and I would have really gotten along, you know, before she got sick. Besides the OCD we have about 249,537 pieces in common now.

BUB

You going a little Rainman on me, kiddo?

JOELLE

I'm just sayin', she and I would have been like this.

(JOELLE moves first to fingers from her eyes to his eyes, back and forth indicating total connection)

I can't believe this is the last of her puzzles and a piece is missing. That's fucked up. Helen would agree with me.

BUB

She'd be beside herself.

JOELLE

She sort of is, I guess…What was the first one we did together… the maple leafs? It was almost seven months ago, you know.

BUB

Yeah. It was May.

JOELLE

Yep. May. Bastard missed our birthday.

BUB

So, your brother and this missing piece here have been on the lam for about the same amount of time. I know you thought he'd be back on his meds by now.

JOELLE

There's still a couple weeks before Jack and Joelle's Orphan Twins Thanksgiving. I'm buying into the miracle bullshit at this point.

BUB

On a positive note, maybe you're not officially an orphan if this author is your pops, eh?

JOELLE

He's dead, too.

BUB

Jeez, kid.

JOELLE

So, Bub, the girl at the desk said the next puzzle is one of those color gradation ones. I hate that shit. It makes me want to stick my head in a microwave.

BUB

Ha. Those have never been my cup of tea either. But, hey kiddo, I think this is my last rodeo.

JOELLE

Your last puzzle?

BUB

Helen's last puzzle, so yeah, last one for me, too. I've never been good at these darned things anyway, and she's getting worse. You need to take a break from this place too. It's not going to make him come around any faster.

JOELLE

I'm going to miss you, Bub.

(JOELLE points at last piece)

Last piece…

BUB

Here you go, kid. You do the honors.

(BUB hands her last piece and grabs his jacket)

JOELLE

(JOELLE unsatisfactorily puts in last piece, shrugs shoulders, picks up her bag and jacket)

So…what are we going to do about the missing piece?

BUB

Miss it, I guess.

(BUB and JOELLE share a knowing glance and walk together toward the Library Exit)

LIBRARIAN

(Announced over intercom)

Denver Central Library is now closed. We'll reopen tomorrow at 9am.

(BLACKOUT)

END.

THE SIDE OF THE ROOM

by Dakota Hill

CHARACTERS:

AARON: Male in his fifties to sixties

SEAN: Male in his twenties to thirties

(—) Represents overlapping dialogue.

SETTING: The living room of a modest but well-kept apartment in the middle of the night.

In the darkness we see a couch down center. A bar upstage left. Books on shelves and stacked in various piles take up a large portion of the space.

Silence.

(AARON enters through the front door. Another man follows closely behind. The second fellow, SEAN, closes the door.)
(AARON turns on a lamp near the couch and illuminates the room in a dim glow.)
(SEAN waits by the door.)

AARON

You can come in.

SEAN

(Taking a few small steps)
Okay. Cool. Thanks.
(Silence. The two men stare at one another for what feels like an eternity.)

SEAN

Is this…I mean, is this okay?

AARON

Of course it is. You wouldn't be here if it weren't.
(A short pause. AARON keeps his gaze fixed on SEAN. SEAN, in turn, looks toward the floor.)

SEAN

You know if I had noticed your wedding ring I wouldn't have come on to you.

AARON

But you did come on to me.

SEAN

Yes.

AARON

And continued after you noticed the wedding ring.

SEAN

Yes. I did.

AARON

Why?

SEAN

Because you're attractive and you seem nice. If not a little intense. Moody, maybe, is the word I want?

AARON

A little intense. I've been told that—

SEAN

But still nice, of course. I didn't mean to imply you weren't nice—

AARON

You didn't—

SEAN

Good. Good. That's good.

AARON

I can be intense.

SEAN

Yes.

AARON

And I like to think that I am nice—

SEAN

That's all I meant.

AARON

Thank you for the accurate assessment.

SEAN

You're welcome.

(The awkward silence returns momentarily. SEAN moves toward a book case and surveys the shelf.)

SEAN

You weren't lying about the books, were you?

(Taking in the entire room)

Wow. They are everywhere.

AARON

I really should donate some of them.

SEAN

You could sell them, couldn't you? Make a lot of money. Or start a book store?

AARON

I think I'd rather give them away. If I ever decide I don't need them, that is.

(Pause)

Do you read a lot?

SEAN

Um…no. Honestly. Not really. I've read plenty of books in my life. It's just that most of them were homework.

AARON

Never for fun?

SEAN

There was one. This guy I dated a long time ago gave it to me. I read that book.

AARON

Giving a novel to someone is a profound act, I think.

SEAN

How's that?

AARON

You don't give someone a novel you don't care about. You give someone a novel that's deeply personal. You're trusting that this someone will appreciate the same world. Will see and feel and revel in all of the same wonders and joys and sorrows that you felt when you read it. And if they don't, you'll have to reconcile what that means. You'll have to work that out between the two of you.

(Short pause)

Which book was it?

SEAN

I'm so bad at remembering titles of books. Or movies. I don't have any retention for things like that, I guess? I remember parts of it. Parts of that book really stuck with me. There's a line toward the end.

(Pause. Recalling.)

"Shine your shoes for the fat woman?"

AARON

Lady. Not woman. Salinger.

SEAN

Yeah, it was.

AARON

Franny and Zooey.

SEAN

Yes, that was it! Shit, that's impressive.

AARON

That one stuck with me for a long time as well.

SEAN

I'm not sure I really understood what he was talking about. But I liked it. It made sense even though it didn't. Does that make sense?

(Laughs)

AARON

The fat lady is all of us and everyone else. You should shine your shoes for the fat lady because she deserves the best of you. Like everyone does.

(Pause)
What happened to this guy you dated once? This guy with wonderful taste in fiction?

SEAN

I wasn't good enough.

AARON

I'm sure that's not true—

SEAN

No, no, I really wasn't. I was a kid. Nothing too dramatic about any of it. Just a dumb kid who didn't realize what he had and didn't appreciate that he wouldn't always be so young and pretty.

AARON

You're still quite young and very pretty.

SEAN

I'm pushing it on both fronts.
(A pause. Sudden and evident discomfort moves over SEAN's face.)

SEAN

This is pretty weird for me. Being here, I mean.

AARON

Did you want to leave?

SEAN

No, no. I didn't say that. I'm just saying—

AARON

What are you saying?

SEAN

Just that—

AARON

That you want to leave? Is that what you were saying?

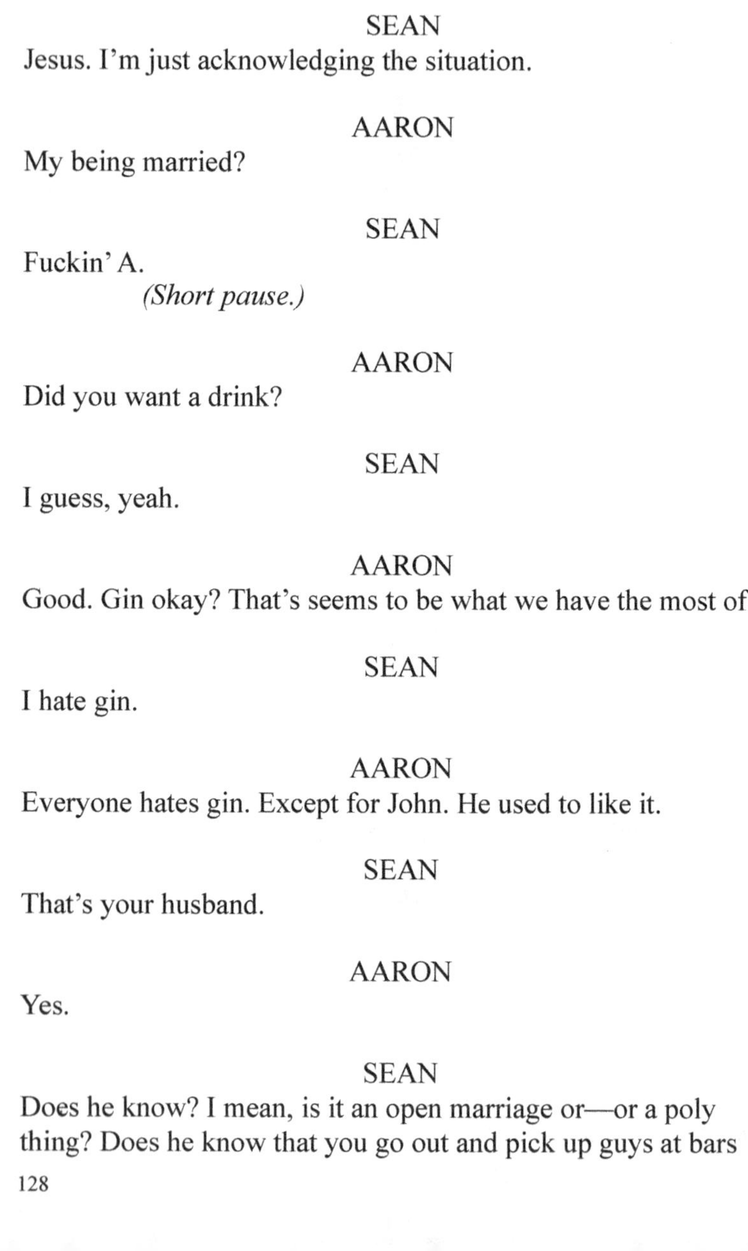

SEAN

No—

AARON

What was it then—?

SEAN

Jesus. I'm just acknowledging the situation.

AARON

My being married?

SEAN

Fuckin' A.

(Short pause.)

AARON

Did you want a drink?

SEAN

I guess, yeah.

AARON

Good. Gin okay? That's seems to be what we have the most of.

SEAN

I hate gin.

AARON

Everyone hates gin. Except for John. He used to like it.

SEAN

That's your husband.

AARON

Yes.

SEAN

Does he know? I mean, is it an open marriage or—or a poly thing? Does he know that you go out and pick up guys at bars while he's out of town?

AARON

He's not out of town. He's asleep in the other room.

SEAN

(All but leaping toward the door.)

I'm sorry?

AARON

He's sound asleep. He sleeps like a dead person. No, he doesn't know that I picked you up. Or that I went out for that matter. But it doesn't matter.

SEAN

Maybe it doesn't to you, but it certainly matters to me. I have to go—

AARON

Why do you have to go?

SEAN

Because I'm not going to fuck you while your husband is asleep in the next room.

AARON

Who says you're fucking anyone? Did I say that I invited you here to have sex with me?

(Pause.)

I'm waiting. When did I say that I intended to sleep with you?

SEAN

I thought it was implied. You invited me back to your house after meeting me in a bar.

AARON

And?

SEAN

After talking to me for all of 25 minutes—

AARON

And?

SEAN

That carries with it a pretty specific implication.

AARON

I said I wanted to go somewhere quiet so I could get to know you.

SEAN

That's what you're supposed to say—

AARON

I meant it. I mean what I say.

(Silence seeps back into the room.)

SEAN

Well, that's—

AARON

Not what you're used to?

SEAN

No. Frankly, it is not.

AARON

I couldn't hear you very well in the bar. I wanted to hear what you had to say. You're pretty. But, I needed to make sure the inside matched the outside.

SEAN

I see.

AARON

Good.

SEAN

You don't want to sleep with me?

AARON

Maybe. But I try not to base my behavior off of my expectations.

SEAN

I respect that.

AARON

You're not disappointed?

SEAN

Yeah, yes, I am actively disappointed that you're married. And I'm actively disappointed that your husband is sleeping mere feet from us.

(Pause)

But, I'm not upset with your honesty.

AARON

I don't have room for anything but complete and total and utterly depressing honesty at this particular junction in my life.

SEAN

(As a joke to himself)

At least I'll always know what to expect—

AARON

For instance, I can't sleep with my husband anymore. I want to. It's not uncommon. Our situation. In fact, I'd venture to say that it is actually fairly common at our age. At his age.

SEAN

And is this his reward for that?

AARON

For what?

SEAN

For being patient with you not wanting him. You go out and pick up guys half your age while he's asleep.

AARON

You don't know anything about it—

SEAN

I know it's pretty shitty any way you swing it. Right? Maybe you want to get caught with someone so you don't have to say it out loud.

AARON

Say what out loud?

SEAN

That you want to see other people, fuck other people. That you've fallen out of love—

AARON

There's something you don't understand. Something that you won't understand until you're standing on the other side of the room, my young friend. I still love him very, very much. He's been my best friend in the entire world, my closest confidant, my absolute and entire everything for as long as I can remember. But, I can't sleep with him anymore and the reasons why are fraught with drama and tragedy. And they aren't the point. I will love him with every single fiber of my being for the rest of my life. Until I die. Both things can be true at once. I can love John and still go out at night.

SEAN

But it doesn't sound like he'd be happy about you actively looking.

AARON

I wasn't looking. Not really. But I saw you and then I spoke with you and you seemed like someone I could sleep with and care about as well. And what am I supposed to do with that newfound information but take you somewhere quiet and affirm my hopes. My desires.

SEAN

(After a pause)

That's a lot, ya know.

AARON

What is?

SEAN

All of that. All of this. You. Okay, you. You're a lot. I didn't expect a complicated situation when I left the bar with you.

AARON

What did you expect?

SEAN

I sort of just thought I was going home with someone with commitment issues who was attractive if not a little older than I usually go for, and that we'd have a nice, decent, if not wonderful time ripping each other's clothes off. And then I'd feel bad for a few days about helping someone commit…ya know…an infidelity and that would be it. You'd disappear into your own life and I would go on with mine. Worst case scenario I'd see you out at a bar or brunch or somewhere and you'd be with someone who was most definitely your husband. And if we spotted each other we would just pretend we were total strangers. Our defense mechanisms would align at the exact same moment and we would form an unspoken pact from across the room. We do not know each other. That night so long ago never happened. And your husband would never be the wiser. I overthink things, I guess.

(A short pause)

AARON

You are definitely overthinking this situation.

SEAN

I think you're under-thinking it. And I-I-I think it's really shitty. What you're doing. You said that you don't have room for dishonesty, right?

AARON

That's right.

SEAN

What in the fuck would you call this? What you're doing right now? What would happen if he walked in on us naked on your couch, huh?

AARON

That's not going to happen—

SEAN

(His voice steadily rising)

What if he beats me to death in a jealous rage and someone at a hospital has to call my mother and tell her that her gay son was beat to death by a jealous husband because her gay son went home with an older, married man because he's going through some weird daddy phase—

AARON

(Laughing)

That's definitely not going to happen—

SEAN

(Shouting)

You don't know that!

AARON

Yes, I do. I am certain that won't happen.

SEAN

(Calming himself. Looking toward the hallway.)

Wow, he really does sleep like a dead person. That didn't wake him up?

AARON

No, that didn't wake him up. It wouldn't matter if it did.

SEAN

Why is that?

AARON

(Moving to pour another drink)

How old do you think I am?

SEAN

I don't know.

AARON

You have an idea, I'm sure.

SEAN

Older, but not old…

AARON

I'm in my late fifties. When I was your age I too had an affinity for older men. John was older, but not old. The truth is older men become old men. That's what happens. You wake up one day and you're old.

SEAN

I don't think I understand.

AARON

My husband is in the other room. Asleep. In a medical bed. With a tube that feeds him. An IV drip that hydrates him. A catheter that allows him to relieve his bladder and a colostomy bag that allows him to relieve his bowels. He's not going to beat you to death because he can no longer walk.

(A long, tense pause)

SEAN

Oh.

AARON

And I can't be honest with him because he can't understand the things I say to him. He doesn't miss me when I'm out at a bar at night, because he doesn't remember me most of the time.

SEAN

Wow.

(Pause)

All those things I said. I-I-I wouldn't have said them if I knew—

AARON

I didn't tell you at the bar because you wouldn't have come with me.

SEAN

I might have.

AARON

But probably not.

(A pause)

SEAN

I'm sorry.

AARON

For what?

SEAN

For your situation.

AARON

Why on earth? I'm the luckiest man in the world.

SEAN

Have you ever…?

AARON

What?

SEAN

I just mean it's a lot to take on. Isn't it?

AARON

Yes, it is. He has people that come and take care of most of it. His doctor. Nurses.

SEAN

Still. It can't be easy.

AARON

Your point?

SEAN

Just that it would be easier to have him looked after around the clock, right.

AARON

He would take care of me if the situation were reversed. I owe him the same. I owe him the very best of myself. I owe him everything I can give.

SEAN

You owe him shined shoes.

AARON

Precisely.

(Silence creeps back into the room. Finally, AARON gives a knowing smile.)

You can go. Really. I won't hold it against you.

SEAN

No, no. I want to stay.

AARON

Why?

SEAN

Because. Because…I just do.

(Silence. AARON moves to a bookcase and searches for a moment. He removes a large hardback novel and hands it to SEAN.)

AARON

I think you should go this time. That way I know you're here with me because you want to be here with me. Not because you feel the need to pity me. You should read that at some point.

SEAN

What is it?

AARON

It's James Joyce. You're going to hate it. But, you'll be better for having read it.

SEAN

Okay. I'll bring it back to you when I'm finished.

AARON

It's yours. It was given to me when I was around your age by someone a little older.

SEAN

It's personal.

AARON

Deeply.

(Silence. The two men look at one another for a long moment before SEAN breaks the trance.)

SEAN

I'll see you later then?

AARON

Sounds wonderful.

(AARON stays put as SEAN moves to the door. Now, the two men are standing on opposite sides of the stage. The distance between is the size of an ocean. SEAN opens the door and is almost gone before he stops and turns back to AARON.)

SEAN

Have a good night.

AARON

You as well…

(With that, SEAN closes the door behind him.

AARON moves back toward the bar to refill his glass.)

AARON

My young friend…

END.

MALUM

A play in one act.

by Ashley Rice

CHARACTERS:

LOU: The extremely well-dressed keeper of the underworld. Satan. The devil. Goes by many names but prefers Lou. Smart and savvy, yet not completely trustworthy. Gender presentation not important. Wears a modern-day suit.

ADAM: The handsome yet vapid first man. Revels in the status quo, fears change. Similar age to Eve. Male-identifying. Wears shades of dark blues and black.

EVE: The beautiful and bored companion to Adam, made of his rib. She is smart, sweet, and a little mischievous. Similar age to Adam. Female-identifying. Wears shades of forrest green and black.

SCENE: A library.

TIME: The beginning.

SETTING: An old-looking library. Just books, no technology. Well-kept but dusty. Stacks of books everywhere, old mugs of half-drunk tea, flowers that have since dried up. There is a large open book on a stand.

AT RISE: LOU is replacing old, dry flowers in a vase with fresh new ones.

LOU

(As if picking up from where they left off, talking to audience)

Malum is an interesting word. It plays a big role in the Judaeo-Christian creation story. You see, as an adjective it means "evil." But, as a noun it means "apple." Years after Genesis was written, clever European interpreters of the ancient writing naturally concluded that the forbidden fruit must have been an apple. But, apples didn't grow in the ancient near-east where the story originated. There are plenty of figs, dates, and grapes. But no apples.

It matters very little, however, what the fruit was. Because it is a metaphor. Obviously. In fact, if you're a Bible literalist you should take your leave now because you are not going to like what I am about to tell you. Which is the truth. Well, one truth. My truth. You see, I was there. I was the keeper of the forbidden fruit. History portrays me as a serpent but keep in mind: history is written by the victors.

(The flower business is done and LOU steps forward to formally introduce themself)

I have a lot of names: Lucifer, Satan, Beelzebub, ruler of darkness. But, I prefer Lou. It fits my demeanor best I think. For those of you who might not be familiar with the Judaeo-Christian story of creation, I'll give you the Spark Notes: God created

ADAM

(Enter ADAM, reacting like he was just created; feeling skin, looking at hands, feet, etc.)

and placed him in Eden, which was pretty much paradise. Waterfalls, flowers, it was honestly exactly what you're picturing. The only rule the big guy had was that

(ADAM looks up, nods)

Adam couldn't eat from the Tree of Knowledge of Good and Evil. More on the tree later. As long as he followed this one rule, he could stay in paradise. After a very short time, Adam got bored. So, God made him a companion and named her Eve.

(Enter EVE, briefly in awe of her own creation, slightly confused. Adam hugs her gratefully)

They got along well, and it was Adam's job to tell Eve the rules.

EVE

What…are we? What is this place?

ADAM

I have no idea, I don't ask questions.

EVE

It's beautiful here.

ADAM

Totally. And all that we have to do to stay is just

(Gestures to stack of books)

not touch that tree.

EVE

Seems reasonable.

(ADAM and EVE move away from center. ADAM plays catch with himself with a pomegranate. Eve arranges the flowers LOU has placed in the vase. She grows more and more bored by the end of the monologue; ADAM does not. He exits eventually, or sits off to the side, eating or playing a game.)

LOU

So, back to this Tree of Knowledge of Good and Evil. God, what a mouthful. Now, you may be picturing, as the authors of Genesis did, an actual tree. But the Bible is full of metaphors, so why wouldn't this be one too? What does a tree become eventually? Fire, sure. A home, absolutely. But also: paper. Every book before you was once a tree. This biblical tree, in reality, was actually the Eden Public Library which contains every book that has or ever will be written. Yes, even the dross that nobody ever reads. We've got a dusty basement full of trashy romances, including the *Twilight* saga. Anyways, before God banished me to the underworld, I was the head librarian of that place. The Eden Public Library, or as most know it by its metaphor, the Tree of Knowledge of Good and Evil. The good-and-evil part is actually a clever literary device called a merism.

(LOU geeks out over these sorts of things)

That's when two opposing words are used to refer to an entirety. So, "good and evil" would simply imply "everything." A tree whose fruits impart the knowledge of everything. It's not a moral thing. Just a building full of literally every book ever. Okay, back to our characters. The first humans. Who, I should also mention for those of you who haven't deduced: aren't literally naked. Another artful literary device. I tried to explain this to my close friends Michelangelo and DaVinci, but they preferred to paint the naked symbolism. Nudity sells, I get it. Anyways Eve quickly grew bored and the more bored she became, the closer she started getting to the library. One day, while I was outside having my smoke break, she got close enough to speak to me.

EVE

Hi there. I'm Eve.

LOU

I know. I'm Lou.

EVE

What is this place?

LOU

A library filled with every book that will ever be written. All the knowledge in the world.

EVE

Whoa.

LOU

Yeah. What brought you over here?

EVE

I…I'm not sure. I feel…something like hunger, but not for food. Something like desire, but not for Adam. And it led me here.

LOU

Come in. Take a look around.

EVE

I can't. One of the first things Adam told me is that in order for us to stay here, in paradise, neither of us can touch this

(Points to stack of books)

tree?

LOU

Paper. Used to be a tree. It's a figure of speech. A metaphor.

EVE

What's a metaphor?

LOU

It's…a way to compare two things that are similar, but aren't really the same. Could also be symbolism, now that I think about it. Doesn't matter. They're books—not an actual tree.

EVE

I think I get it.

LOU

So, God told you you can't touch these books, huh? Sounds about right.

EVE

What do you mean?

LOU

Let's just say homeboy prefers to be the smartest guy in the room.

EVE

I see. Actually, I've never spoken to God. He told Adam the rules before I was created.

LOU

I see. Well that's unfortunate.

EVE

Yeah. A dead end I guess.

(LOU sees the longing in EVE, the one she can't quite describe)

LOU

So, Adam said the rule is that you can't touch the books, but did he say you couldn't consume them?

EVE

How would one go about consuming without touching?

LOU

Have a seat.

(EVE sits and LOU opens a book. EVE lays and listens as if to a story while LOU tells audience)

And so it went for quite some time. Eve would meet me here, and I would read the books of the world to her. Books on sciences, mathematics, literature. We devoured it all, together.

(LOU gets up from their reading, moving aside, leaving EVE laying there in wonder but still not touching any books)

It wasn't until we got to *The Feminine Mystique* by Betty Friedan that Adam started to notice.

ADAM

(Off)

Hey Eve? Babe! Grab me a pomegranate from the west garden and slice it up for me.

EVE

(Simply)

Nah.

ADAM

(Off)

What?

EVE

I don't want to.

(Enter ADAM, confused)

ADAM

Eve. Get me a pomegranate. Please?

EVE

(Simply)

No.

ADAM

But I asked nicely.

EVE

So?

ADAM

So, it's good manners.

EVE

(Laughing gently)

I don't care.

ADAM

Well, I didn't want to have to go there but you have to. You are my wife, you are subservient to me. I tell you what to do.

EVE

Not anymore.

ADAM

What has gotten into you?

EVE

I've been…learning.

ADAM

What? No! At the Tree of Knowledge?

EVE

Yeah. It's actually not a tree, it's a library. The tree is actually a metaphor for—

ADAM

Why would you do that? Why would you want to do that? It's perfect here, and you're going to get us kicked out! And what the hell is a metaphor?

EVE

We're not going to get kicked out, I've been following the rule: I haven't touched a single book. The librarian reads them to me.

ADAM

No, God said not to eat from the tree. I think that means reading, listening, touching, all of it.

EVE

You told me that I just couldn't touch it.

ADAM

Then, I don't know, I told you wrong.

EVE

Oh. Well. Then it's actually your fault. And it's too late now.

ADAM

Damnit, Eve.

EVE

Well, God hasn't noticed yet. Maybe he won't.

ADAM

(Dripping with sarcasm)

Yeah sure, it's not like God is everywhere and all-knowing or anything. He's GOD for Christ's sake.

EVE

Don't be like this. Come with me and see.

ADAM

No.

EVE

Experience knowledge with me.

ADAM

I don't want to. I have no desire to.

EVE

It's incredible, it seems like the more I learn the more I realize how much I don't know.

ADAM

Sounds terrible.

EVE

It isn't. There is so much more than this little paradise.

ADAM

I like this little paradise.

EVE

You're living in blissful ignorance.

ADAM

Yeah, sure. But it's blissful.

EVE

Come with me. I'll have Lou read us one of my favorites.

ADAM

I'm not going to like it.

EVE

Come on. Give it a chance.

(EVE leads ADAM to a relaxing position near where LOU sits.)

LOU

Eve chose one of her favorite books and I began reading. *Romeo and Juliet*. She was fascinated by their acts of love and disobedience. An amateur choice, but, give her a break. Adam fell asleep before the prologue was over.

(LOU goes back to reading. Eve is rapt; Adam is in a deep sleep)

…A glooming peace this morning with it brings;
The sun, for sorrow, will not show his head:
Go hence, to have more talk of these sad things:
Some shall be pardon'd, and some punished:
For never was a story of more woe
Than this of Juliet and her Romeo.

EVE

(Wiping tears)

Every time.

(EVE nudges ADAM awake.)

Are you serious?

ADAM

What?

EVE

You fell asleep?

ADAM

Yeah. That was terrible. The language was weird.

EVE

It's beautiful writing.

ADAM

I don't know. I guess I just prefer story over flowery language. Something to keep me engaged.

EVE

How was that not a story?

ADAM

Well, for starters, it wasn't funny at all.

LOU

Well, we do have the luxury of having every book ever written. What interests you, Adam? What would entertain you?

ADAM

Do you have anything on the Big Bang Theory? I hear that's pretty good.

(Laugh track plays)

LOU

(Making their way over to a large open book on a stand. The Bible)

Ah, yes. Formulaic tropes that insult our intelligence. Great choice.

(Laugh track plays)

ADAM

Huh?

(Laugh track plays)

LOU

Nothing.

(LOU looks over the open book.)

Ah shit.

EVE

What's wrong?

LOU

It counts.

ADAM

What counts?

LOU

My reading to you. It counts.

EVE

So, we broke the rule?

LOU

Oh yeah. God was taking a nap. His sabbath siesta if you will. He didn't notice till now.

(Skimming Bible)

Looks like you're about to get kicked out of paradise.

(Eve smiles slightly)

ADAM

Damnit Eve!

(Laugh track again; this time Adam is not amused)

LOU

(Still skimming Bible, more excitedly now)

To be fair, this book was droll before. Now it's…wow, we changed the course of history. Originally it was just one chapter: "Adam and Eve were created and lived in paradise." Now? Now there's so much more.

ADAM

This is so unfair, I didn't want this. I didn't ask for this.

EVE

Will there still be books? In…not-paradise?

LOU

Oh yes. And you'll have the free will to access them.

EVE

Great.

LOU

It's not going to be easy, but I think it'll be worth it.

EVE

Will we ever see you again?

LOU

Oh hell yeah.

EVE

Perfect.

LOU

Not perfect. But, better I think.

(EVE smiles. LOU steps forward. ADAM and EVE freeze.)

LOU

So, who is to blame? Or, rather, who is to thank? Scholars are still arguing to this day. And that to me is beautiful. Because of Eve, because of this curious woman, humans have traded a life of blissful ignorance for access to divine knowledge. For the ability to read, learn, and debate. Though, that's not to say that some people don't still long for blissful ignorance.

(ADAM dons a MAGA hat)

But don't worry, that option is still available to you if you want it. But for those of you who don't:

EVE

You're welcome.

(BLACKOUT)

END.

About the Contributors

Public Service Announcement
by Theo E.J. Wilson

Theo E.J. Wilson is a founding member of the Denver Slam Nuba team, who won the National Poetry Slam in 2011. He began his speaking career in the N.A.A.C.P. at the age of 15, and has always had a passion for social justice. He attended Florida A&M University, where he obtained his B.A. in Theater Performance. He returned to Denver and is now the executive director of Shop Talk Live, Inc. The organization uses the barber shop as a staging ground for community dialogue and healing. After viral video success beginning in 2015, Theo grew his social media following to well over 68,000 people. Due to audience demand, he published his first book in 2017, *The Law of Action.* The book addresses some of the misconceptions about the law of attraction, and the role direct action plays into manifestation. It can be found on Amazon.com, or his website, TheoWilson.net. In 2017, his TED Talk entitled, "A Black Man Goes Undercover in the Alt Right," was seen worldwide, amassing a total of over 12 million views. He has been featured on BuzzFeed, CNN, Good Day Canada, and TV One.

A Pocket Full of Dandelions
by Kristen Adele Calhoun

"The role of the artist is to make the revolution irresistible." These words from Toni Cade Bambara guide **Kristen Adele Calhoun**'s work as a playwright, performer and organizer. She is the founding program director of ArtChangeUS and co-producer of InterFest, an intersectional arts and ideas festival that began at the Harlem School of the Arts. She is the assistant editor of *Contemporary Plays by Women of Color*, and her play, *Canfield Drive*, about Ferguson, the murder of Mike Brown and the revolutionary power of healing in the face of oppression, had a rolling world premiere in 2019 at the St. Louis Black Rep and The National Black Theatre Festival. Other plays include *Black Cypress Bayou*, *The Oldest Town in Texas*, *Quilombo* (5280 Artists Coop), *With These Hands* (Black American West Museum), and *Ain't Gonna Let Nobody* (NAACP). A native of Dallas, Texas, she is a graduate of the University of North Texas and the Mason Gross School of the Arts at Rutgers University. Kristen is currently reading, writing and living in Accra, Ghana.

Holy Couch
by Edith Weiss

Edith Weiss has been involved in the theater as actor, director, and playwright. Her plays for young audiences and her comedic murder mysteries have been performed locally at the Arvada Center and internationally as far afield as Kazakhstan, Malta, and South Africa. Her work is published by Dramatics, Pioneer, Eldridge, Brooklyn and Big Dog Publishers. Twenty years as a touring stand-up comic informs her comedic style. She was head writer and director of *Vox Phamalia*, an original comedic sketch comedy show produced by the Phamaly Theater Company of Denver (previously the Physically Handicapped Amateur Musical Actors League), starting with *Tales From the Crips* to *Pity Pity Bang Bang* seven years later. Her short adult plays have received productions in Boston, Chicago, NYC, Albuquerque, Kansas City and Denver. *Holy Couch* was shortlisted for the Short + Sweet playwrighting competition in Australia.

Marginalia
by Jeffrey Neuman

Jeffrey Neuman is an award-winning playwright whose work has been performed at theaters and festivals across the United States, Australia and the United Kingdom. He is a Heideman Award Finalist, cofounder of Rough Draught Playwrights, an inaugural fellow of the Denver Center for the Performing Arts Playwrights' Group, director of programming for the Denver Post's Pen & Podium Literary Series, and Colorado's Regional Ambassador for the Dramatists Guild of America. Find him online at www.theaterbyjeff.com.

Outside the Room
by Theatre Artibus, Grapefruit Lab + Larry Mitchell

Grapefruit Lab is the combined vision and multimedia intersection of the work of **Julie Rada**, **Miriam Suzanne** and **Kenny Storms**. Grapefruit Lab's name, derived from Yoko Ono's quip that a grapefruit is the hybrid of a lemon and an orange, encapsulates our goal of combining highly aesthetic, compelling artistic work with work created with and alongside communities in ways that matter. We want to make art without assumptions—art that humanizes and entertains and challenges and brings you into conversation.

Founded by **Meghan Frank** and **Buba Basi, Theatre Artibus** is a Denver-based theatre company and performance space dedicated to strengthening community through the experience of live performance. We aim to be a hub in Denver for intimate, original performances that explore important social themes and for building community through shared space, inspired learning and creative play across disciplines. More info at www.theartibus.com

Larry Mitchell is a freelance unemployed playwright, foodmaker, and teaching artist with too many student loans and no concrete sense of direction or purpose, but he remains hope-infested and is having a good enough time. He shares a two-bedroom condo-partment in Aurora, Colorado, with his witty life partner and a teenage joy-bomb.

Toxoplasmosis
by Sean Michael Cummings

Sean Michael Cummings is an actor, writer, comedian and theatre artist working in Denver, Colorado. Writing: *Toxoplasmosis* (Denver Center), *Bazaruto* (Phamaly). Awards: Best of Westword, Denver Center True West, The Orchard Project Fellowship (NY). Acting: *The Rough* (Catamounts); *The Nina Variations* (Boulder Ensemble Theatre Company); *Twist Your Dickens* (Aurora Fox); *As You Like It* (Colorado Shakespeare Festival); and many others. Sean is a proud member of the BETC Writer's Group and holds a BA in Performing Arts from Colorado State University. Find more information at booksean.com. He is represented by Big Fish Talent. *Toxoplasmosis* is dedicated to Mom and Tre.

Something to Read at the End of the World
by Maureen Biermann

Maureen Biermann has a bachelor's degree in Theater from Northwestern University and a master's degree in Geography from Penn State. She has worked as an actor, director, and producer in Michigan, an English teacher in Austria, a climate change adaptation researcher in Tanzania, and a college instructor in Alaska and Colorado. She currently coordinates an Arctic policy program in Alaska. She spends most of her time parenting her two young kids, supporting progressive change, reading books, and thinking about what she would write if she had the time, with the hope that eventually she will just sit down and do it. She lives in Glenwood Springs, Colorado.

The F Word
by Claire Caviglia

Claire Caviglia graduated from the University of Denver in 2019 with a degree in hospitality management. She especially enjoyed attending DCPA's playwriting classes during her time in Colorado. First published at 19, Claire has had one-act plays performed across the country. Most recently, her ten-minute play *Night with No Stars*, was included in *Clockhouse Journal*. Claire is now working in hotel management in California.

The Missing Piece
by Christina Miller + Addie Levinsky

Christina Miller is an Oxford MBA and business consultant who is in the process of opening Marfa Meats, a local abattoir and butcher shop in Far West Texas. She's currently obsessed with food security, sustainable agriculture, the desert, bird identification, the influence of anonymity on interactions, and small-town newspapers.

Addie Levinsky is a Colorado native who spends her days bringing a creative and human element to the tech world, in addition to writing. Most of her free time is spent partaking in Type 2 fun on bikes or running on dirt, adventuring, reading, and hanging out with her mini aussie. In her next life, she wants to live off the grid and be a novelist...and a stand-up comedian.

The Side of the Room
by Dakota Hill

Originally hailing from West Texas, **Dakota Hill** has been acting and writing in Denver for over ten years. He was last seen on stage in The Lulubird Production of *The Mrs. Wheatland Pageant* and Vintage Theatre's production of *The Boys in The Band*. His play, *The Spare Room*, premiered as a part of Vintage Theatre's first new play festival and then produced by MadLab Theatre in Columbus, Ohio. His play, *Burnt Offering*, was the premiere play produced at Theater29 in Denver as well as his play, *You'll Find Flies*, which premiered in June of 2019. Dakota would like to thank his amazing partner, Brandon, for his unwavering support.

Malum
by Ashley Rice

Ashley Rice is a performer, writer, and comedian from Pittsburgh, Pennsylvania. She has been in many plays and improv shows all over. Ashley has a few degrees hanging on her wall, including a BA in Journalism and Political Science, and an MFA in Acting. She is also an ABA-trained paralegal, believe it or not. She lives in Denver, Colorado, with her husband Wayne and their sweet little dog Jet.

CPSIA information can be obtained
at www.ICGtesting.com
Printed in the USA
BVHW030514071220
594980BV00004B/21

9 781733 988728